A SERIES OF
NEW TESTAMENT
STUDY GUIDES

# PASTORAL LETTERS

## HELPS FOR
## READING AND UNDERSTANDING
## THE MESSAGE

Bob Young

# James Kay Publishing

## Tulsa, Oklahoma

A Series of New Testament Study Guides
PASTORAL LETTERS
Helps for Reading and Understanding the Message
ISBN 978-1-943245-54-3
Second Edition

www.bobyoungresources.com

www.jameskaypublishing.com
e-mail: sales@jameskaypublishing.com

# *Table of Contents*

# *Preface to the Series*

A number of factors have converged in my life as influences on my method of Bible study and Bible teaching. My undergraduate training in Bible and biblical languages served as the foundation for 25 years of full-time preaching ministry. During those years in ministry, I periodically took graduate coursework in an effort to stay fresh.

When I decided to pursue graduate education diligently, I already loved teaching from an exegetical viewpoint while paying special attention to the historical-cultural context and the grammatical-syntactical features of the biblical text. I had seen the healthy ways in which people respond to thoughtful efforts to explain and apply the message of the Bible. I had developed the habit of using that same kind of Bible study in my sermon preparation. For those reasons, I focused my graduate training in ministry dynamics and how to integrate academic studies with practical applications. Because I did graduate work while continuing full-time work in ministry, I was blessed to have a laboratory to apply and test what I was learning.

My years of teaching and administration in Christian higher education coupled with increased involvement in the world of missions have made me even more aware of the need to view the Bible, insofar as possible, outside one's own social, cultural, experiential, and religious backgrounds. My interpretative efforts today are influenced by my training and experience. I try to understand the biblical context, the historical-cultural context, and the literary context—vocabulary, genres, grammar, and syntax. I try to understand the original message of the author and the purpose of the text as first steps toward understanding the message of the text in today's world. I want to know what the text said and what it meant, so that I can know what it says and what it means today.

As I have prepared these study guides, I have constantly asked myself, "What would I want in a study guide to the biblical text?" I have been guided by this question, at times excluding technical details and academic questions, at other times including such items because of their value in understanding and communicating the text. Above all, I have tried to provide a practical study guide to put in clear relief what the text says as a first step toward valid interpretation of what the text means and how it should be applied today.

I wrote these guides with multiple readers in mind. There is little new in these volumes, but preachers and Bible class teachers will be helped with their study and review of the text. Christians who have an interest in the message of the Bible will be helped by the textual jewels and the summaries that are included. The initial motivation to prepare these volumes came from my desire to provide a resource that will be translated into Spanish, keeping in mind the needs of preachers, Bible teachers, and Christians who do not have access to the many resources and books that exist in English. A good way to describe these guides is that they are simple explanations designed to help with the task of understanding and applying the biblical text. A few technical details are included to help with understanding, to identify repeated words or themes, and to give insights into the message of the text. May God bless you in your desire and your efforts to understand and apply the message of the Bible!

# Introduction to the Series

**The Purpose of These Guides**

To describe the publications included in this series as "Bible study guides" says something about their intended purpose. As guides, these little books do not attempt to answer every question that may arise in your study of the biblical text. They are not commentaries in the strictest sense of the word. The focus of these guides is distinct.

I have as a primary goal to encourage you to do your own study of the Bible. This series of study guides is designed to assist the Bible student with preliminary and basic exegetical work, and to suggest some study methods that will enrich your study and help you identify the message of the text—whether in a specific verse or paragraph, a larger context, or an entire book of the New Testament. A primary goal of these guides is to help you maintain a focus on the purpose and message of the original author. The message of the original writer should inform our understanding of the text and its application today. One should not think that the message and meaning of the text today would be significantly different than the message and meaning of the original document.

The title also says that these guides are "helps." I have tried to provide resources to guide and enrich your study, keeping the purpose of the original author in view. This desire has informed the content of these study guides. Many study guides exist and there is no need to write more books that basically have the same content. Generally, the information included in these guides is designed to help identify the purpose of the original author and the message of the Bible. In some passages, the information included in these guides will provide insights not readily available in other resources.

**What Kinds of "Helps" Are Included in These Guides?**

These study guides reflect how I organize and understand the text of the Bible, taking into account various exegetical factors such as syntax, grammar, and vocabulary. Along the way, I share some observations that will help clarify passages that are difficult to understand. I have not tried to comment on every passage where potential problems or differences in understanding exist. I have not noted every textual variant in the original text. At times these notes may seem to be unnecessary comments on passages where the meaning is clear; that probably means I am trying to share insights to deepen understanding and appreciation of the text. In other passages, some may ask why I have not included more comments or explanation. Such is the individualized nature of Bible study. The overall goal of my comments is to help maintain a focus on the original author's message and purpose for writing—the "what it said and what it meant" of the original author in the original context.

For each chapter, there is a "Content" section that usually includes a brief outline, followed by notes ("Study Helps") about the biblical text. The content sections of these guides, including how the text is divided and how paragraphs are described, are drawn from my own reading and analysis of the text and from a comparison of several translations. In only a very few cases does the outline provided in this guide vary from the majority opinion, and those cases are noted and the reasons given. In some chapters, there is an overview with introductory comments to help orient the student to the overall content and message of the chapter. In a few chapters, there are some additional observations. Often, a paraphrased summary is included as part of the textual notes or in a separate section after the study helps. As noted above, the comments are not intended to answer every question. In a few cases, I have addressed topics that are not treated in detail in other resources. Texts that are easily understood and matters that are customarily included in other resources are, for the most part, not treated in detail here.

## A Useful Tool for Understanding the Message of the Bible

While the primary purpose of these guides is to assist in personal study of the biblical text, these guides will also serve the casual reader who wants to understand the basic message of the Bible. The guides are written in such a way that the reader can understand the general message of the text, along with some interesting and helpful details, simply by reading the guide. One might describe theses guides as a kind of "CliffsNotes" to the Bible, but they are intended as helps and should not be thought of as taking the place of Bible reading and Bible study.

**How to Use This Bible Study Guide in Personal Bible Study**

This guide is not intended to take the place of your own Bible reading and study but is intended to provide insights and suggestions as you read the Bible, and to be a resource that will help you check your understanding. **You are encouraged to use this guide and your own Bible side by side.** Some sections of this guide may be difficult to understand unless one can identify the specific part of the text that is being described or explained.

**No specific translation of the biblical text is included in this guide**. Two goals influenced the decision not to include a translation of the biblical text. First, it is hoped that you will be encouraged to use your own study Bible. Second, these notes are designed to be helpful in biblical study regardless of the version the reader may prefer for personal Bible study.

My primary purpose is to make it easier for you the reader and student to analyze and understand the text. Ultimately, you are responsible for your own interpretation of the Bible and you cannot simply follow what a favorite preacher or commentator says. Often the study notes for a chapter or subsection of a chapter are followed by a brief summary of the content, focusing on the message.

Five Steps for Bible Study. The suggested process for effectively using these Bible study guides involves five steps. First, you should read an introduction to the book of the Bible you wish to study. The introductions provided in these guides will serve well. They are for the most part briefer than normal and do not cover every detail. In this series of guides, sometimes one introduction is provided to cover multiple books, as in the case of the Thessalonian correspondence and the Pastoral Letters.

The second step in your study is to read through the book of the Bible you wish to study to understand the overall content. It will be helpful if this can be done at a single sitting. The student facing time constraints may have time for only one reading, but multiple readings will reveal additional details of the book, providing you an opportunity to notice repeated words and phrases and to think about the message of the book, how the book develops its message, and how various parts of the book are connected. You will find help for your reading in the chapter outlines that are provided in these study guides.

Now you are ready to begin your study of individual chapters or sections. The process is simple: read a section of the text until you have a good understanding of it. This is not an in-depth reading to resolve every question but is a general reading to understand the contents of the passage.

The fourth step is for you to write your own outline of the chapter or section, with paragraphing that reflects major thought patterns, divisions, and topics. In these study guides, each chapter has a section with suggested paragraphing based on a comparison of various translations. While it is possible to skip this step in which you do your own analysis and paragraphing, and to move directly to the paragraphing provided in the study guide, this is not the recommended approach. You will benefit from taking the time and investing the energy to do this work in initial reading and understanding.

Finally, the study guides have a section of study helps that will help you read and understand the text and keep the intent of the original author in mind as you do more focused study. In many chapters, a final section that summarizes the message of the chapter is included.

## Initial Reading and Paragraphing

In other articles and publications, I have explained the importance of preparatory reading and personal study of the biblical text. In the five-step process described above, initial reading and paragraphing occur in the second, third, and fourth steps. When the student carefully works through these steps, it becomes clear that this is a "Bible" study and is not simply a process of reading more background information and commentary from a human author who is trying to explain the Bible. Although many students jump immediately from reading an introduction to reading a commentary, it is important that the student learn to read and study the Bible for herself or himself. Once the biblical text is familiar, I suggest the student think about the themes that can be identified and how to mark the paragraph divisions, based on the content of the passage and the subjects treated. Once this work is complete, it is good to compare the resulting paragraphing with that of several versions, or with the outlines in the content sections of these guides.

## A Note About Paragraphing

Paragraph divisions are the key to understanding and following the original author's message. Most modern translations are divided into paragraphs and provide a summary heading. Ideally, every paragraph has one central topic, truth, or thought. Often, there will be several ways to describe the subject of the paragraph. Only when we understand the original author's message by following his logic and presentation can we truly understand the Bible. Only the original author is inspired—readers must take care not to change or modify the message. A first step toward integrity with the text is to develop the ability to analyze it and establish paragraphs.

*Note: This introductory information is not repeated for each chapter. Students will find it helpful to return to this introductory section again and again to guide their study, especially before beginning the study of a new chapter of the Bible.*

## A Few Other Matters

No footnotes are included in these Bible Study Guides. Comments that are often included in footnotes have been inserted parenthetically into the text. Since I have worked primarily from the biblical text, language tools, and my own notes, no bibliography is supplied.

As I began working on the series of Bible Study Guides and worked on the preparation of my notes, I found that the studies written by Dr. Bob Utley reflected much of my own training, and the ideas and concepts I had developed about how to approach the biblical text. My appreciation for his work is apparent at times in my explanations of some texts and in some of the concepts, thoughts, and wordings I have used. Some phrasing may reflect his treatment of the text, but I am responsible for the contents of these guides.

I am grateful for the teachers and professors who taught me to love the text and helped me develop the skills that make the study of the Bible a rich experience. I want to thank those who have encouraged me to put my teaching style in written form. These study guides reflect much of what I would share in teaching a Bible class. The written materials do not include the applications I would make of the text, but applications must always be contextualized.

Finally, I am grateful to my wife, Jan, for her support and encouragement in this endeavor. Writing requires time, and the office time I have invested has meant less time spent with her.

# A Word About Formatting

The format of the Study Helps in each chapter follows the outline that is provided for the chapter. The major points of the outline are used to begin new sections of the Study Helps. Biblical references that introduce sections or subsections of the Study Helps are placed in bold type to assist the student. In the case of paragraphs that cover multiple verses, the biblical references are placed in progressive order on the basis of the first verse in the citation.

Standard abbreviations of biblical books are used. Verse citations that do not include the name of a book (e.g. 2:14) refer to the book being studied. Abbreviations that may not be familiar to some readers include the following: cf. = compare; e.g. = for example; v. = verse; vv. = verses.

The first time a translation is mentioned, the standard abbreviation is included for translations that are less well-known. Subsequent references use only the abbreviation.

Greek words are placed in italics. Often, the corresponding Greek word, a literal meaning, and other translation possibilities are placed in parentheses immediately after an English word. Greek words are written as transliterations in English letters, using the basic lexical form of the word. It is hoped that this will make it easier for the reader without a knowledge of Greek. Many readers will find these references interesting, especially in those passages where there is repeated use of the same Greek word. Readers can quickly pass over this inserted parenthetical information if desired.

In a few cases, parentheses are used to indicate Greek verbal forms or noun forms where this information would be significant to the student with some understanding of grammar. The Greek language uses three classes of conditional statements: clauses that begin with "if." These constructions are noted when the use is significant. The first class condition is assumed to be true from the viewpoint of the author. The second class condition is contrary to fact. The third class condition is hypothetical. Again, the reader can pass over this information rapidly if desired.

The Greek text used is the 27th edition of *Novum Testamentus Graece* which is identical with the 4th revised edition of *The Greek New Testament*.

Quotation marks are often used to call attention to special words or topics, and also to indicate citations or translations of the biblical text, most of which are my own. This is done to help the reader identify references to the biblical text, since no specific translation of the biblical text is included in this Study Guide.

Parentheses are used liberally to enclose information and comments that would often be included in footnotes. It is hoped that readers will find this more convenient, both those who want to read the expanded explanation and those who wish to skip over the parenthetical material.

Comments concerning contemporary applications of the text are limited, but are included from time to time.

Summaries are provided for many chapters, with the goal of helping to make the message of the chapter clearer. Some of these summaries are paraphrases, some are written in first person, from the standpoint of the author; others are written in third person and are explanations of the content. Summaries written in either the first person or third person are not translations and they are not paraphrasing. They are attempts to communicate the basic points and the purpose of the original message.

# *Introduction to the Pastoral Epistles*

Because of their content, the letters Paul wrote to Timothy and Titus are often referred to as the Pastoral Epistles, especially with reference to their instructions about church leadership. However, even a casual reading will identify several other primary themes. Any effort to understand the message of these letters must begin with the question, "What was the purpose of the author in writing the books we know as Pastoral Letters?" To answer that question, one must also seek to understand the situations he addressed.

## Locations and Dates

Several specific geographic locations are mentioned in the letters. (1) Timothy to remain at Ephesus when Paul went to Macedonia (1 Tim. 1:3); (2) a later visit to Ephesus by Paul is mentioned (1 Tim. 3:14); (3) Paul mentions being in Asia and Rome (2 Tim. 1:15-17); (4) Paul had been at Troas (2 Tim. 4:13); (5) a visit to Miletus, and considering a parallel construction in the verse, a visit to Corinth (2 Tim. 4:20); and (6) a visit on Crete (Tit. 1:5). From the text of the letters, we know that Timothy was at Ephesus and that Titus was on Crete when they received the letters.

These internal geographic references in the Pastorals do not fit nicely into the chronology of Acts and Paul's other letters. If the first reference above is a part of the third missionary journey, the second does not fit since Paul chose not to go to Ephesus but only to greet the elders from Ephesus on Miletus (Acts 20). Obviously, Paul had already visited Rome (or was in Rome) when he wrote these letters according to the third reference, but a visit to Rome does not occur in Acts until the end of the book. Acts and the other letters of Paul have no reference to a visit to Crete and describe Titus as involved in other travels. Paul wrote in the book of Romans about his desire to visit and minister in points west of Rome, even to Spain, so as not to build on another's foundation.

As a result of these factors, and based on church tradition, many believe that Paul was released from the Roman imprisonment mentioned in Acts 28 and continued to travel (sometimes described as a fourth missionary journey), until he was arrested, imprisoned again, and eventually killed around the year AD 68. Clement, near the end of the first century, wrote of Paul's release. Eusebius also mentions Paul's release. This means that the Pastoral Letters fit into the time frame of the 60s after the events of Acts 28, where we learn that the Roman imprisonment lasted at least two years. Based on internal references, the book of 2 Timothy is usually assigned a date near the end of Paul's life.

There are no internal references to the date of the book of Titus. The book is included in the Pastorals along with 1 and 2 Timothy due to vocabulary (and the similar subjects of 1 Timothy and Titus), because of the focus on false teachers, and perhaps because the visit to Crete does not fit into the chronology of Paul's ministry and the other biblical references to Titus. There is nothing in the biblical text to demand a late date. Crete was near enough to locations visited during Paul's other travels that he could have gone there with Titus on a visit not recorded by Luke in Acts. Titus is sometimes described a young man, but considering his activities during the ministry of Paul, and if the speculation that Titus could have been a brother to Luke is correct, Titus could easily have been approximately the same age as Paul.

The following provides a timeline of Paul's life with approximate dates (AD) and locations along with an indication of where events fit into the timeline of Acts. As noted in the comments above, the Pastoral Epistles likely belong the time period after the book of Acts since internal references in the books do not fit into the Acts narrative.

| Date | Location | Bible Text | Letters Written by Paul |
|------|----------|-----------|-------------------------|
| 50 | Jerusalem assembly | Acts 15 | Gal, 1-2 Thess written around this date |
| 51-52 | Paul in Corinth 18 months | Acts 18 | |
| 53-56 | Paul in Ephesus 3 years | Acts 19 | 1-2 Cor, Rom written during this time |
| | Overland trip | Acts 19-20 | |
| 58-60 | In Jerusalem and Caesarea | Acts 21-26 | ("a little over 2 years") |
| 60-62 | First Roman Imprisonment | Acts 27-28 | wrote Eph, Phil, Col, Philm |
| 63-66 | Additional travels | after Acts | wrote 1 Timothy, Titus |
| 66-68 | Last imprisonment | after Acts | wrote 2 Timothy |

**Author**

  An extended study of the authorship of these books is beyond the scope of this introduction. The text of the letters mentions Paul as author. None of the factors that have been cited in opposition to Pauline authorship are beyond reasonable explanation in the context of what we know of first century history. These studies are written from the viewpoint of Paul's authorship.

**Recipients**

  While the letters bear the name of specific individuals who were Paul's coworkers in ministry, the letters were written to be read in the churches. This is seen in the plural final greetings, the formal introductions, and various internal references that include a wider audience than Timothy and Titus. Timothy was in Ephesus when Paul wrote the letters to him. Titus was on the island of Crete when he received the letter from Paul. A history of these two evangelists and their locations will inform our understanding of the message and Paul's purpose in writing.

  <u>Timothy</u>. From the time that Paul encountered Timothy on the second missionary journey (Acts 16), Timothy was a faithful and loyal helper to Paul as they worked together in the missionary expansion of the church. They established a relationship of confidence and friendship that was never ruptured. initially a relationship between mentor and learner, afterward it appears that they became coworkers so that Paul, anticipating his death, wrote with the goal of passing on many aspects of the ministry to Timothy. Timothy is mentioned frequently in the book of Acts (17:14-15; 18:5; 19:22; 20:4) and in ten of Paul's thirteen letters (Rom. 16:21; 1 Cor. 4:17; 16:10; 2 Cor. 1:1; Phil. 2:19; Col. 1:1; 1 Thess. 1:1; 3:2, 6; 2 Thess. 1:1; Philm. 1; and of course, in the two letters that were directed to Timothy). From the book of Acts and these references in the letters, we can reconstruct the following. Timothy traveled with Paul at least as far as Corinth (Acts 18), helping with the development of the Thessalonian church. Timothy was with Paul when Paul wrote Romans and the references in 1 Corinthians suggest at least one trip by Timothy to Corinth, possibly two, to help resolve difficulties. Timothy may not have traveled with Paul to Jerusalem

(Acts 18-19), but not long after Timothy was with Paul in Ephesus, and Paul sent him on ahead (Acts 19:22) before Paul traveled to Macedonia and Achaia, returning through Macedonia (Acts 19-20).

Several years later, likely after the Roman imprisonment, Paul and Timothy were together again in Ephesus, and Paul left Timothy there when he traveled into Macedonia, charging him to guard against deviations from the sound words and sound teaching of the gospel, thus addressing a problem that had begun to penetrate some of the Christian communities. This false teaching had several elements (see below under Purpose).

Ephesus. The church in Ephesus was the result of the visit of Paul along with Priscilla and Aquila (Acts 18). Paul returned to Ephesus after visiting Jerusalem and spent about three years there (Acts 19). The gospel echoed forth into Asia Minor from the base that Paul established in Ephesus. During this initial period of no more than three or four years, elders (the same group of leaders were also called bishops and pastors) were established in Ephesus, as evidenced by Paul's desire to meet with them briefly as he traveled from Macedonia with haste to arrive in Jerusalem (Acts 20). In that meeting with the Ephesian leaders, Paul predicted that problems would arise from within the leadership. When Paul wrote the first letter to Timothy some four or five years later, giving clear instructions about the selection and appointment of bishops, those instructions should be understood against the background of a church that was encountering challenges doctrinally with the present of false teachers, and the likelihood that some of the problems had arisen from those serving as bishops.

Titus. It is believed that the conversion of Titus was the result of Paul's preaching in Antioch of Syria. Paul mentions Titus in three of his letters (Gal. 2:1, 3; 2 Cor. 2:13; 7:6-7, 13-14; 8:6, 16, 23; 12:18; and 2 Tim. 4:10). Acts does not have any reference to Titus, despite the fact that Titus was Paul's faithful companion, and that Paul assigned to Titus some tasks that were delicate, both in Corinth and on Crete. Titus was a Gentile.

Crete. Little is known of the development of the church on Crete. Jews from Crete were present on the Day of Pentecost (Acts 2) and would have returned home having heard the gospel.

This presents the possibility that the church was established shortly afterward. What can be known with certainty is that the church on Crete had some deficiencies, was encountering false teaching especially from a Jewish element, and that Paul charged Titus with the task of naming leaders in the church. Of interest is that Paul sent a Gentile to help solve a problem with a Jewish element in the church.

## The General Purpose of the Pastoral Letters

Understanding how the Pastoral Letters fit into the chronology of the New Testament is important for determining what was happening in the churches in terms of doctrine and teaching, leadership, and church development. Although the book of 1 Timothy addresses church administrative and organizational matters such as worship, leadership, and the function of various groups within the church, the first chapter mentions as primary the need to combat false teaching. Paul mentions the need for healthy church function in 1 Tim. 3:14.

Written in a historical context at a time when Paul was anticipating his own death, a clear focus of 2 Timothy is the need for Timothy to endure suffering and hardship as he assumes a greater role in the mission work, but one can also identify several references to false teachers.

A part of the work of Titus on Crete was to appoint leaders to help deal with some opponents within the church (Tit. 1:5-9). The admonition to appoint leaders includes the need to correct first some things that were lacking or had been left undone. In addition to these admonitions, one sees in Titus frequent references to false teachers and false teaching. The presence of false teachers demands capable church leaders who can serve effectively. Other topics in the book of Titus include the importance of keeping the believers busy in the work and the need to organize the work and worship of the church so that the false teachers are not given an opening.

These brief summaries suggest that a common purpose of the Pastoral Letters is to address the presence of false teachers in the church. This purpose is seen in the contents of the teaching, the organizational instructions, and the desire to give both Timothy and Titus authority. Very early in church history, some in the churches desired to deviate from the form of the apostolic teaching known as the kerygma. The false teaching described in the Pastoral Letters appears to have elements of Roman philosophy, Judaism, and perhaps some early Gnosticism. All three of the Pastoral Letters have a strong emphasis on sound words, sound teaching, doctrine, and godliness.

## First Timothy

**Purpose of the Letter**. The letter was written to Timothy to advise him on his teaching and ministry to the church. This letter includes instruction about doctrine (and the necessity of opposing false teachings), behavior, organization, discipline, and relationships. The false teachings probably included a pride in knowledge, an attitude which failed to address behavior and resulted in both decadence and false asceticism. The purpose of the letter likely includes to encourage Timothy in his work and teaching at Ephesus (1:3-7), to guide the leadership and conduct of the church (3:14-15), and to instruct Timothy in his ministry (chapter 4, esp. 4:13-16) and his relationships in the church (5:21). A final charge to Timothy urges the practice of the principles outlined (6:11-16, 20-21).

Paul is concerned about ministry with relation to the gospel message, the church, the church leaders, and the minister (in this case, Timothy himself).

**Contents of the letter**. The contents of the letter can be understood through the lenses of various themes or topics. (Numbers in parentheses refer to chapters.)

- How the church should function. The church's teachings and lifestyle (1), the church's conduct (2), the church's leadership (3-4), the church's conduct (5), and the church's teaching (6).
- Sound doctrine is to be proclaimed and practiced. Protect and proclaim the message (1), instructions about the behavior of the church (2), the leaders of the church (3), the minister and ministry in the church (4), instructions related to various groups in the church (5), and the need to practice the principles of the message (6).

**Theology of the Letter**. The letter presents interesting theological descriptions which may reflect confessions or songs of first-century Christians.

- God. 1 Tim. 1:17, "To the King of the ages, immortal, invisible, the only God, be honor and glory forever and ever. Amen."
- Salvation. 1 Tim. 2:3-6, "This is good, and it is pleasing in the sight of God our Savior, who desires all people to be saved and to come to the knowledge of the truth. For there is one God, and there is one mediator between God and men, the man Christ Jesus, who gave himself as a ransom for all, which is the testimony given at the proper time."
- The mystery of godliness. 1 Tim. 3:16, "Great indeed, we confess, is the mystery of godliness: He was manifested in the flesh, vindicated by the Spirit, seen by angels, proclaimed among the nations, believed on in the world, taken up in glory." Jesus appeared in body, was authenticated by Spirit, was seen by messengers, preached among nations, believed on in world, ascended out of this world. Note the parallelism, resulting in three sets of two—appeared and was preached, was authenticated and believed on, was seen and then ascended. Note also that this is the "center" of the book of 1 Timothy.
- Jesus Christ. 1 Tim. 6:15-16, "which he will display at the proper time—he who is the blessed and only Sovereign, the King of kings and Lord of lords, who alone has immortality, who dwells in unapproachable light, whom no one has ever seen or can see. To him be honor and eternal dominion. Amen."

**Chiastic Outline of the Book.** Analyzing the contents of a book is easier when one looks at the book as a whole. Below is a chiastic outline that suggests some of the parallel sections and connections that can be identified in the book of 1 Timothy. The word chiasmus is from the Greek letter *chi* (X) and simply means that the outline is in the form of the letter *chi*. Another way to describe this kind of outline form is that it resembles an arrow. In a chiastic outline, the focal point is at the center, at the tip of the arrow.

A possible chiastic outline for 1 Timothy could look as follows:

1_Introduction, Initial Charge to Timothy: Regarding Teaching and False Teachers
    2_Charge regarding All Members: Prayer and Behavior in Worship
    *[This charge guides Timothy's work with and instruction to the church]*
        3_Charge to Develop and Work with Leadership in the Church
        *[This charge contains semi-public instruction about church leaders]*
            **Purpose Statement: How to act in the church [3:14-4:5]**
            *[The nature of the church, the purpose of the church, the mystery and foundation of the church, threats that surround the church]*
        4_Charge to Integrity in Ministerial Leadership
        *[This charge to Timothy concerns his personal life in ministry]*
    5_Charge regarding All Members: Relationships in the Church [5:1-6:2]
    *[This section gives instructions concerning various groups in the church, their responsibilities and Timothy's interaction with those groups]*
6_Closing, Charge to Timothy: Regarding Teaching and False Teachers

In this outline, Chapters 1 and 6, "Charges to Timothy," introduce and conclude the book, and the principal theme reflected in the purpose statement is in the center, at the point of the arrow. The brief descriptions of the contents of the chapters show a general correspondence between the chapters: 1 and 6, 2 and 5, 3 and 4.

Outlines of entire books are usually not provided in the introductory sections of these guides. This outline is provided to demonstrate the unique structure of the book of 1 Timothy and to demonstrate the process of analyzing an entire book, searching for a primary theme and trying to understand how the various chapters or sections of the book relate to that theme.

## Second Timothy
**Purpose of the Letter**. The letter was written to Timothy near the end of Paul's life. It reflects Paul's final instructions to his son in the faith and serves as a final testament of faith, although it is doubtful that Paul had this in mind as a purpose of writing.

- To give Timothy specific instructions to come to Paul, to give Timothy a ministerial mandate

- To help Timothy deal with specific problems that confronted the church.
- To write indirectly to the Ephesian church and to encourage it.

**Contents of the Letter.** The contents of the letter can be seen as follows: as a historical and personal call to action, as teaching focused on the gospel, as principles for ministry, and as a charge to Timothy. Here are summaries of the four chapters showing how these four possibilities can be applied.

Historical and Personal Challenge to Action
- What you have received
- The importance of doing something with what you have received
- The power for action in such a time as this is from God
- The result of faithful action

The Gospel in 2 Timothy
- Chap. 1: Battling for the Gospel
- Chap. 2:1-13: Suffering for the Gospel
- Chap. 2:14-26: Working for the Gospel
- Chap. 3: Defending the Gospel
- Chap. 4: Preaching the Gospel

Four principles set forth in the letter
- Effective ministry is generation to generation
- Effective ministry is urgent
- Effective ministry depends on God's power
- Effective ministry which incorporates these basic characteristics has the desired result

The Charge to Timothy
- Be faithful to the Word
- Be faithful to your Ministry
- Be faithful to your People

**Literary Themes and Concepts in the Letter.** Themes of special importance in the letter include the following.
- Gospel, message, sound doctrine
- Deposit, commitment

- The subtle nature of godlessness and faithlessness
- Metaphors to describe the church and Christians

## Titus

**Purpose of the Letter**. The purpose of the letter can be seen by surveying the letter section by section.

- 1:5, <u>to correct things deficient and to appoint leaders</u>. This verse seems to present the primary purpose of the letter, although one may identify other indications of the purpose as one reads the letter.
- <u>To emphasize the importance of effective leadership in combatting false teaching</u>. How is this importance reflected in the letter? Note the following: (1) the importance and reason for leaving Titus on Crete, 1:5; (2) the qualifications or characteristics of the elders/bishops, 1:6-8; (3) the work and responsibility of the leaders, 1:9; and (4) teaching that leads to a healthy faith, 1:13.
- <u>To make clear the nature of the opposition on Crete</u>. The nature of the opposition, false teachers, 1:5; 2:1,5-6,15; 3:9-11; characteristics of the false teachers, 1:10-16, 3:9-11.
- <u>To present and encourage healthy teaching</u>. References to doctrine occur in 2:1, 7-8 , 15; 3:9. The wider focus on doctrine includes (1) instructions about faith and conduct, (2) the repetition of the phrase, "sound doctrine," (3) two summaries of Christian doctrine, 2:11-14; 3:4-7, and (4) instructions for various groups in the church, 2:1-10 (especially in 2:1, 2, 8).

**A Primary Theme of the Letter.** The phrase, "that which is good," appears in 1:8, 16; 2:3, 7, 14; 3:1 ,8, 14. The study of Titus should include an effort to discern the meaning of this phrase in the context of the letter.

**Outline of the Letter.** This outline sets forth the principal sections of the letter.

- 1:1-4 Salutation, greeting
- 1:5-16 The importance of naming leaders of sound doctrine in view of the challenges and the opposition

- 2:1-10 The importance of teaching various groups in the church about sound doctrine
- 2:11-14 First doctrinal summary
- 2:15 Therefore, teach, reprove, exhort....
- 3:1-2 The importance of the Christian life in the public arena
- 3:3-7 Second doctrinal summary
- 3:8 Therefore, emphasize this
- 3:9-11 Final summary and warning concerning the opposition
- 3:12-15 Conclusion

# 1 Timothy 1

*[Note: it is suggested that the student read the introductory materials in this guide before beginning any individual preparatory reading and analysis. Students are encouraged to become familiar with the five steps of effective Bible study.]*

## CONTENT

The paragraphing included in the Content section of each chapter are merely suggestions or guides. The student is encouraged to identify the paragraphs, and subsections within each paragraph, to assist in his or her own study. The division of the biblical text into paragraphs is usually fairly standard in modern translations.

Outline of the Chapter

| | |
|---|---|
| **1:1-2** | Greeting, salutation |
| **1:3-11** | Timothy is admonished to defend the truth against false teaching |
| **1:12-17** | God's mercy is evident in Paul's life |
| **1:18-20** | The importance of Timothy's responsibility |

Overview of the Chapter

The entire first chapter serves as an introduction to the letter, giving details of Paul's charge to Timothy. (See the outline of the book of 1 Timothy in the Introduction.) The theme section states the purpose of the letter (1:3-11) and is followed by a doxology (1:12-17). The charge to Timothy is repeated in 1:18-20.

## STUDY HELPS

**1:1-2.** As was customary in first-century letters, the salutation identifies the writer (Paul, apostle) and the recipient (Timothy, child in the faith). Perhaps Paul describes himself as an apostle to emphasize his authority. Timothy is described as a son (literally, child) to Paul with regard to Christianity. The phrase does not mean physical son or that Paul had baptized Timothy (see

1:18; see also Acts 16 where it appears that Timothy was already a Christian when Paul first encountered him).

The phrase "God our Savior" is unusual (see Tit. 1:3), but does not present new theological understandings. The saving work of God the Father in Jesus Christ was a shared work of the Godhead so that both Father and Son are designated as "Savior" in the New Testament. The reference to Jesus as our hope is also unusual.

**1:3-11.** When Paul left for Macedonia, he left Timothy in Ephesus to combat false teachings. Timothy was to "instruct" (*paraggello*) certain persons not "to teach something different" (*heterodidaskaleo*). In the context, the instructions refer to a different doctrine. The characteristics of these false teachers and their teachings show both Jewish and Greek influences, as reflected in the descriptions of the teachings. These teachings included false doctrine, myths and fictitious stories, various interminable genealogical matters, speculations that led to controversies and arguments, a desire to focus on Old Testament law, empty talk, and conceit. The teaching was strange (different) and led to undesirable results. The antidote is love from a pure heart, good conscience, and sincere faith, which things are the goal of all sound teaching.

**1:8-11.** These verses are one long sentence is Greek and point to the value of the Law in defining morality and moral living. The Law is good, but only if used appropriately. The Law is not designed to provide a legalistic doctrinal set to guide righteous people in godly living. The focus of the false teachers on observing the Law missed the purpose of the Law. The Law was not given for the righteous person—think of the "just who live by faith," but for the lawless and disobedient and those who practice things contrary to sound (healthy) doctrine. The Greek word for "healthy" or "sound" is the word from which we get our word hygiene. Healthy doctrine should be evaluated not only on the basis of content but also on the basis of results. The result of sound doctrine is holy living as much as correct teaching. The context makes clear that sound (healthy) doctrine is related to lifestyle and is consistent with the gospel. It is possible to live a life contrary to sound doctrine. Sound doctrine is not only what is taught; sound doctrine is reflected as much or more in how one lives. This text is one of only four uses of this phrase, "sound doctrine," in the New Testament (see 2 Tim. 4:3; Tit. 1:9, 2:1).

**1:12-17.** In these verses is Paul's doxology (word of glory or word of praise) for how Christ Jesus had intervened in his life even when he was opposing Christianity (Acts 9:1-2). An introductory doxology was part of the usual letter form in the first century. Paul affirms that his ignorant actions were a significant force against Christianity, but that the Lord's grace was abundant, great enough to bring faith and love into his life in Christ Jesus.

---

*Faithful is the saying and worthy of all acceptance: that Christ Jesus came to the world to save sinners of whom I am foremost.* 1 Timothy 1:15

---

**1:15-16.** In v. 15 is the first of five "faithful" sayings: Jesus Christ came to save sinners. These sayings are used to introduce and point to key teachings in the Pastoral Letters (1:15; 3:1; 4:9; 2 Tim. 2:11; Tit. 3:8). Paul's point is that no one needed saving more than he. Paul marvels that God wanted to save him and that God was able to use him. The greatness of Jesus' mercy and grace in Paul's life gives hope to all. In the context, one should note that Paul identifies himself with the false teachers; he himself was formerly an opponent and false teacher.

**1:17.** This verse concludes the section with a glorious doxology. The entire first chapter serves as introduction.

**1:18-20.** The command (v. 18) likely refers back to 1:3. Timothy is to fight (*strateuomai*) against the false teachers who are described as rejecting faith and a good conscience so that their own personal faith is shipwrecked. Two specific names of false teachers are mentioned. Hymenaeus is mentioned again in 2 Tim. 2:16-17. This Alexander is unidentified elsewhere in Scripture. This Alexander would probably not be the Alexander of Acts 19 and 2 Tim. 4:14, since the Alexander mentioned here was formerly of the faith, and Alexander the metal worker seems to have always been an unbeliever.

## The Message of the Chapter Summarized

The church in Ephesus was established in the first half of the sixth decade AD, that is, in the early 50s. A few years after the establishment of the church in Ephesus, Paul was there with his coworker Timothy. When Paul decided to go to Macedonia, he left Timothy in Ephesus. At some later time, Paul wrote to Timothy. This writing is the letter we know as 1 Timothy.

"I remind you of what I told you when I left you in Ephesus. You need to oppose the false teachers because they are leading people away from love and faith in Christ. They bring in theories, myths, genealogies, speculations, and try to show how well they understand the Law as they try to integrate it into the Christian faith. They totally misunderstand that the Law is for the wrongdoer and not for godly people. It is true that the Law opposes all kinds of evil actions, but healthy teaching opposes the same actions, and other evil actions as well, because they are not consistent with the teaching we have received, teaching that points to the glory of God in the gospel.

"I understand how the gospel opposes evil. The gospel has the power to change people. I am the best example because I was the worst of sinners. God through the gospel has chosen me for his service and given me strength, even though I did terrible things. My experience demonstrates the power of the gospel—Jesus came to save sinners! I know that fact personally and I am Jesus' example of the power and glory of the gospel. Only the King of all time periods, who lives forever beyond this visible realm and is in fact the only God, deserves honor and glory!

"I remind you again of your responsibility, Timothy. Wage the battle, maintain the faith firmly with a good conscience. When people reject the healthy teaching of the gospel, they wreck their own faith, just as Hymenaeus and Alexander have done. I am hopeful that the problems that they have now will help them see the truth so they will not speak against God."

# 1 Timothy 2

*[Note: it is suggested that the student read the introductory materials in this guide before beginning an individual preparatory reading and analysis.]*

## CONTENT

The outlining and paragraphing included here are only a suggestion. The student is encouraged to identify the paragraphs and subsections within each paragraph in his or her own reading and study. The division of this chapter into paragraphs is fairly standard in modern translations. The descriptions of the paragraphs (often given in a heading that introduces the paragraph) vary in many translations. The descriptions vary depending on how the first-century context in which the instructions were given is understood.

<u>Outline of the Chapter</u>
The outline of 1 Timothy that was included in the introduction shows that the contents of Chapter 2 relate to shared activities of the church, especially in prayer and worship. These instructions are usually understood as having primary reference to the assemblies.

| | |
|---|---|
| **2:1-7** | Prayer (general instructions; possible applications in the assembly) |
| **2:8** | Men (proper attitude in prayer; everywhere, including the assembly) |
| **2:9-15** | Women (behavior, attitudes, and attire; also related to the assembly) |

## STUDY HELPS

**2:1-7.** "First of all," is Paul's way of putting things in order. The phrase often means "of first importance" as opposed to suggesting the first of several points. Paul exhorts (*parakaleo*, to beseech, to urge, to encourage) them. Prayer is to be offered for others (literally, all men, *anthropos*, here with the meaning of all people, everyone), but especially for governmental leaders (kings, but by extension rulers, those who govern). God is concerned for the salvation of all, and Jesus died for all (vv. 3-4). Paul was sent to the Gentiles to help with the inclusion of "all." The purpose of praying for governmental leaders is so Christians can live peaceful and quiet lives (v. 2) in holiness and dignity. Note the four different words used to describe prayer: petitions (*deesis*), prayers (*proseuche*), intercessions (*enteuxis*), and thanksgivings (*eucharistia*). All of these can be used and are appropriate in prayers for others and for self, both in private prayer and in public prayer settings.

**2:3.** The phrase "God our Savior" is repeated from the salutation. Prayers offered for others are pleasing to God.

**2:4**. God desires the salvation of "all men" (*anthropos*). The word includes both males and females and means all people. Salvation is only possible by knowing the truth. The order of the verbs (to be saved, to come to a knowledge of truth) does not indicate a sequence but a single concept.

**2:5-6.** Jesus in his service as mediator is described as "the man." NET prefers to translate as intermediary, since mediator has a specific use in contemporary English and could possibly lead to misunderstandings concerning Jesus' role. Jesus is not a mediator in the sense that the word is commonly used today. Jesus is a capable go-between, representing and connecting both God and man. Jesus can serve in this way because he is divine, but he also took on human nature and participated in the human experience. The connection between God and humanity is through "Jesus the man"—Jesus who was himself human. Jesus as mediator (cf. Hebrews 8-9) brings to his role both his divine nature and his human nature.

**2:8.** The reference to men in this verse uses a word that is specific to the males (*aner*). Another word (*anthropos*) is usually translated man but refers to humanity, both male and female, as in vv. 2, 5, and 6. The phrase "in every place" or "everywhere" may eliminate an exclusive application of this verse to public worship settings. The phrase could be applied very broadly; it could also be applied to several house churches in different places in the city of Ephesus.

Paul's instructions to the men includes one verb modified by a prepositional phrase, "to lift holy hands without anger and disputes." Despite the grammatical construction, translations of this verse often describe three behaviors that are associated with acceptable prayer: lifting holy hands, without anger, without disagreements or arguments. Lifting hands in prayer was a common Jewish practice. Lifting holy hands is interpreted by some as meaning holy living; that is, the emphasis is not on lifting hands but is on lifting <u>holy</u> hands. Drawings in the catacombs show Christians with upturned hands, possibly indicating a posture of openness and an attitude of receiving more than of giving. The instructions of this verse likely have little relationship to the often-observed practice in contemporary churches of arms fully extended upward. Lifting hands in this context relates only to the men as they are leading in prayer. Anger is likely a reference to personal relationships more than relationship with God. Dissension (disputes) refers to disruptive actions and argumentation between human beings (cf. Rom. 14:1-2). Paul's focus is on the attitude of prayer.

**2.9-15.** The use of "likewise" to introduce a new group will occur again in 3:8 and 3:11. After the men are admonished toward proper behavior and attitudes in prayer (without anger or arguments), the women are instructed to demonstrate in their lives appropriate dress, attitudes, and behaviors. The most obvious application is in the context of the assembly although the principles can easily be applied to other public settings.

**2:11.** In the text of 2:9-15, the number of the noun changes from plural to singular and back to plural (women in vv. 9-10, 15b; woman in vv. 11-15a). This change is key to understanding this passage. Some translations connect the last phrase of v. 10, "with good works," with v. 11. The use of the singular noun beginning in v. 11 does not prohibit an application to all Christian women, but the context may suggest a specific application to a married woman in relation to her husband.

I fear that we read this text through twenty-first century eyes and fail to hear it clearly. "All submission" may be better than "full submission." In the contemporary world, we abhor submission and forget that Jesus was submissive, that all are called to submission to God, and that all Christians are called to mutual submission as a part of being filled with the Spirit (Eph. 5:21). That a woman was receiving instruction in the church was an advance over Judaism where she was forbidden to study the Law or attend school.

**2:12-14.** The verb "to have authority" (Greek, *authenteo*) is not easy to interpret; in this verse is its only occurrence in the New Testament. The word is usually defined as domination or acting on one's own authority (without proper authority). The concept of quietness appears twice in vv. 11-12. The word "quiet" (*hesuchia*, silence) modifies submission in v. 11, and is applied to learning and teaching in v. 12. The verb that comes from the same root appears in 1 Thess. 4:11 and seems to refer to attitude more than absolute silence. The adjectival form of the same word appears in 1 Tim. 2:2 with reference to every Christian. The context here does not suggest that the named actions are acceptable if done with the proper attitude—not domineering. The modifier moves the meaning in the opposite direction.

An analysis of the text shows that the limiter is not related to the teaching or manner of teaching; the limiter is the "whom"—the persons being taught. As noted above, the singular may suggest that the question has to do with how a wife and husband should interact in the public assembly. How does a woman show respect for her husband (Eph. 5:33)? Remember that both Ephesians and 1 Timothy were addressed to the church in Ephesus.

Paul's illustration based on Adam and Eve may support the husband-wife relationship application. The argument is theological, based on the consequences of the events in the Garden and God's instruction that the woman's desire will be for her husband (Gen. 3:16). Perhaps the basis of the instruction is that the women were more susceptible to the false teachers (2 Tim. 3:6-9). Paul notes that Eve was created after Adam as his helper, that Eve was the one deceived, and that Eve was also the one who fell into transgression. Two consequences were assigned to Eve: submission to her husband and pain in childbirth.

**2:15a.** Translations of this verse often ignore the grammatical number (singular or plural) of the pronouns. The singular continues in the first part of this verse. Here is the literal reading: "she (the woman, Eve) will be saved (delivered, protected) through bearing children." The use of the singular in the first half of the verse maintains the close connection of this verse to Gen. 3:13, 16.

**2:15b.** With Eve as the model or representative of all women, the second part of the verse returns to the plural number: "if they continue in faith…."

**2:9-15.** If the paragraph with the singular number noun or pronoun (2:11-15a) is treated as a complete parenthetical thought that has as its purpose to illustrate Paul's point, then the reading of the text is something like this (2:9,10,15b).

> …*likewise, also that women should adorn themselves in respectable apparel, with modesty and self-control, not with braided hair and gold or pearls or costly attire, but with what is proper for women who profess godliness with good works—if they continue in faith and love and holiness, with self-control.*

The ESV suggests this connection between v. 10 and v. 15 with hyphens, setting off the section of text (2:11-15a) that is illustrative.

> …*but with what is proper for women who profess godliness—if they continue in faith and love and holiness, with self-control.*

This passage has been the source of much controversy and even division in the church and deserves close study in an effort to understand the message of the book.

### The Message of the Chapter Summarized

In a chapter that seems to be addressed to the church as much as to Timothy, we find instructions about the Christian life, especially as it relates to prayer. The references to personal interactions suggest an application in the context of the assemblies of the church.

"First of all, we ought to be using petitions, prayers, intercessions, and thanksgivings as we pray for everyone. It is especially important to pray for governmental leaders and those with authority, so they will let us live in peace, quietness, godliness, and dignity. Such prayers please God because he wants everyone to be saved and to know the truth. Jesus gave himself for everyone and is still our intermediary with God. The message of salvation about faith and truth is the message I preach to the Gentiles, which serves to remind you of how much God wants everyone to be saved.

"Men should pray with holy hands and without anger and quarrels.

"Women should dress respectably, not ostentatiously. It is fitting that they demonstrate modesty and self-control that reflect godliness through good works—if they continue in faith and love and holiness with self-control.

"A woman (wife) should learn quietly and submissively, not teaching and exercising authority over a man (her husband), but exhibiting quietness. This instruction is based on Adam's creation first, and Eve's creation as his helper. Adam was not deceived; Eve was deceived and she transgressed. Her transgression was not beyond God's ability to save. She will be saved through child bearing.

"So, the women should continue in faith, love, holiness, and self-control."

# 1 Timothy 3

*[Note: it is suggested that the student read the introductory materials in this guide before beginning an individual preparatory reading and analysis.]*

## CONTENT

The paragraphing included in the Content sections is intended only to give suggestions or to serve as guides. The reader is encouraged to identify the paragraphs and subsections within each paragraph as part of his or her own reading, analysis, and study. In this chapter, the division of the biblical text into paragraphs is usually fairly standard in modern translations, although a question exists as to how 3:11 fits into the instructions in 3:1-13.

Overview of the Chapter

**3:1-13**, the first part of this chapter lists three different types of ministry: bishops (3:1-7), deacons (3:8-10, 12-13), and women (3:11). The best possibilities for applying the instructions concerning the women (v. 11) are (1) to the widow's role (5:9-16), or (2) to a group of women servants (compare Rom. 16:1).
**3:14-16**, the second part of the chapter is brief; it explains Paul's desire to revisit Ephesus and the importance of advancing the work of the church and the message of the gospel.

Observations about the Chapter

Given the overall emphasis of the book on combatting false teachers, this chapter should be understood in the context of the false teachers' lifestyle and teachings.

To see where this chapter fits into the overall structure of the letter, refer to the outline of the book in the Introduction. In general, this chapter contains instructions to Timothy about his work with bishops, deacons, and some women servants in the church. The goal is to understand proper activity in the church, given the fact that Paul's intended visit may be delayed.

## STUDY HELPS

**3:1-7.** The first group addressed in this chapter is the bishops (*episkopos*, overseer, bishop). The use of "likewise" sets off the different groups that are addressed in this chapter, as it did in 2:9.

---

*Faithful is the saying: when anyone desires the oversight, he has his heart set on a good work.* 1 Timothy 3:1

---

**3:1.** In this verse is the second of five "faithful statement" sayings in the Pastoral Letters. The first class conditional clause assumes truth. In this kind of construction, the "if" can often be translated as "when" or "since." Paul says that serving in church leadership, specifically as a bishop or overseer, is a good work. If problems had arisen within the leadership in the church at Ephesus, some may have been questioning the value of having leaders. In this context, Paul is saying that serving as an overseer is a good work, despite the fact that problems had arisen. The value and importance of having leaders who want to lead is obvious, but this verse does not seem to rise to the level of giving a requirement or establishing a hard and fast rule for serving as a leader. Certainly, this verse does not exclude a potential leader simply because he would prefer not to serve.

"When someone aspires to or desires to serve as a bishop, the work he desires is good." Many faithful Christians have served as church leaders when it would have been easier, and they would have preferred, not to serve. Paul speaks more than once of his compulsion to preach, and Jesus prayed about the difference between his human will and the will of the Father. One can easily imagine a scenario something like this: "I would prefer not to serve, but I recognize the need and that God has put me here at this time, so I will serve." Is a person with such a humble spirit automatically disqualified from service? I think not. Again, the construction of the text does not set forth a requirement.

The reference here is to bishops or overseers. I will use "overseer" to translate *episkopos* from this point forward in these study notes, primarily because the word bishop carries some baggage and the possibility of being misunderstood in the contemporary religious world. It is interesting that the book of 1 Timothy does not use the term elder with reference to a church leader until Chapter 5 (but see in 4:14 a reference to the group of elders). Other passages make clear that the terms bishop or overseer, elder, and pastor all refer to the same ministry (5:17; Acts 20:17, 28; 1 Pet 5:1-2; Titus 1:5, 7).

**3:2.** The phrase "husband of one wife" is difficult to interpret. At least four possibilities have been advanced: (1) it is a reference forbidding polygamy, (2) it is a reference to remarriage after divorce, excluding such persons from the role of overseer, (3) it refers to a second marriage after the death of the first wife, and (4) it is a way of saying a man must be faithful and attentive to his wife. The same phrase is applied to a certain group of widows (5:9); it should be noted that in the context of 5:9 the younger widows were urged to remarry (5:14). Of the four possibilities listed above, it is hard to understand how the first would apply as a unique requirement for serving as an overseer since polygamy would not be permitted to any Christian. The fourth possibility likewise applies to all men in the marriage relationship. The second and third are obviously informed by problems that face the contemporary church more than by the known historical setting in Ephesus. To dogmatically claim perfect understanding seems unwise in view of the ambiguity of the phrase. We read the phrase through contemporary eyes and seek to apply it to situations that are probably beyond the concerns of Paul in Ephesus. Concerning questions such as the continued service of an elder after the death of his wife and a number of other situations where this verse is often cited as proof, it seems the better answer is that the Bible does not say.

**3:2-7.** The church at Ephesus had overseers (also called elders) as early as Paul's meeting with them as recounted in Acts 20:17ff. The date of the book of 1 Timothy, probably about five years after Acts 20, suggests that the instructions in this passage may be corrective. If problems had arisen from within the eldership as Paul predicted in Acts 20, it may be that Timothy was charged with guiding the church through the process of selecting additional or new leaders.

Since the Pastoral Letters are occasional literature, written for a specific time, place, and purpose, one must beware of the too frequent tendency to press together the instructions in this text with those in Titus 1:5-9, arriving at a single list of characteristics or qualities to be applied in every situation. Such an approach does not reflect how these texts functioned in their first century context, and it is not a valid way to understand the specific messages of these texts. One must consider why some characteristics mentioned in 1 Timothy 3 do not appear in Titus, and vice versa. Since some of the characteristics mentioned in this text and in Titus 1 are not measurable, I prefer not to use the word requirements. These are characteristics or qualities of God's leaders.

Regarding Paul's reference to the "children" of the overseer (3:4), see my comment on 5:8, where I explain why the use of the plural includes the singular. The qualities given here present few if any difficulties in interpretation. The "trap of the devil" in v. 7 presents two possible interpretations: a trap laid by the devil, or the same kind of trap that ensnared the devil. No internal factors in the text give reason to prefer one over the other, but I like the second: it is easy to become proud, fall into disgrace, and be rejected by others, just as occurred in the fall of Satan.

**3.8-10, 12-13.** Deacons are not mentioned in 2 Timothy or Titus, but in Phil. 1:1 it appears that a defined group of servants existed and that they were called deacons. Some have seen a reference to the first deacons in Acts 6, but that the Seven were deacons in an official sense is not clear in the text of Acts 6. The word deacon means servant or minister; the etymology of the word suggests menial service. The New Testament does not define the role and function of these specially designated servants. The word deacon suggests they are servants and not administrators.

The paragraph begins with the word "likewise." This word is used to introduce a new group, distinct from the overseers of 3:1-7. The qualifications for the deacons are not as extensive as those for overseers, and one notes some repetition.

**3:9.** The reference to the "mystery of the faith" has confused some. If the word "mystery" is understood as the inclusion of both Jews and Gentiles in the church (cf. Eph. 2:11-18; 3:1-6), then the reference may be explained as a willingness to serve everyone. This verse presents a case where a consistent translation of a specific Greek word serves better than the dynamic equivalence method that tends to use synonyms. For example, consider the NIV translation, "deep truths of the faith." What are the deep truths of the faith? The parallel use of the word "mystery" in Ephesians is helpful to our understanding of this passage in 1 Timothy, given the fact that Ephesians and 1 Timothy were written to the same church in the same general time frame.

**3:10.** The reference to prior testing or approval is also puzzling. If vv. 9-10 are understood as a unit, the meaning is to prove the willingness of the deacons to serve everyone with humility. Defining the reference in this way seems helpful to me.

**3:11.** This one verse that is inserted into the context of the deacons—note that references to the deacons continue in vv. 12-13—has been the source of no little trouble and speculation.

The verse (3:11) begins with "likewise." The Greek syntax thus suggests the introduction of a new group. The construction is parallel to v. 8 where a new group, the deacons, is introduced. I conclude that v. 11 also introduces a new group of church servants. Who are these women? They are certain designated women servants. Some translations have the word wives, but this translation is doubtful. The Greek does not have two different words for woman and wife so the meaning must be determined by the context. Other translations have deaconesses, but had Paul wanted to say deaconesses, the feminine form of the word he used in v. 8 was available. Paul did not write "deaconesses." One must work with and explain the word "women."

The early church had women in various servant roles. Women are described as servants in Rom 16:1 and Phil. 4:3. Paul mentions various women by name in Romans 16. Later in this letter (1 Timothy 5), Paul describes the widows—a special group of older women servants. One can easily imagine church ministry settings where a male deacon would be incapable of serving effectively, or that his service in some circumstances would be inappropriate. On the basis of v. 11, the qualifications or characteristics for this group of female servants were similar to those for male servants. Remember that we are talking about servants. Our contemporary understanding of this text too often focuses on a specific church office and depends on exercising some kind of official authority.

The possibility that this verse is a reference to the widows (5:3-16) has been largely overlooked. Against the possibility, one can argue that the group of widows has not been introduced previously in 1 Timothy. However, the recipients of the letter would have been well aware of the existence of the special group of widows. In the context, Paul was not instructing Timothy to organize new groups of servants. Thus, when Paul refers to the women, a reference to the widows could have been a normal understanding. The use of the word "widows" in 3:11 would not have been appropriate because not all widows were included. By using "women" as the parallel to "deacons" Paul refers to women servants, a group apparently known to the Ephesian church. The church in Ephesus would not have faced the same interpretative problem we face today. They knew what Paul was talking about!

Based on the instructions given in Chapter 5, those added to the widow's roll were to be over 60 years old with no family. A widow in this group had been the wife of one husband and remarriage was not anticipated. This understanding of the marital status of the women would explain why Paul addresses the characteristics of the women servants in v. 11, and then returns to the men servants with teachings in vv. 12-13 that would not apply to the women. In summary, v. 11 builds on vv. 9-10, applying the same concepts to the women servants. Besides the things mentioned in vv. 9-10, in vv. 12-13 are mentioned some things that apply to the deacons but not to the women servants.

Seeing in vs. 11 a reference to the women servants (widows) who are mentioned later in the context is natural. Some have noted evidence for female servants (deaconesses?) in post-biblical church literature. However, in parallel, also in post-biblical literature are references to regional bishops who had authority over a specific region. The references to such bishops show how quickly the church moved away from the biblical teachings and practice. Is such also possible in the case of the later references to deaconesses? Perhaps the most generally acceptable option is to understand v. 11 as a reference to various female servants. However, limiting the reference to the group of widows explains the construction of the paragraph (3:8-13), and why Paul in vv. 12-13 returns to the specific marital situation of the male servants.

It is very unlikely that v. 11 refers to deacons' wives or to overseers' wives. A reference to deacons' wives might explain the construction with v. 11 inserted in the paragraph focusing on deacons. It does not explain how or why one would connect v. 11 with the instructions concerning overseers (vv. 1-7). And, it is not clear why the deacons' wives would have such qualifications when none are given for the overseers' wives.

---

### Paul's Purpose in Writing to Timothy

*I hope to come to you soon, but I am writing these things to you so that, if I delay, you may know how one ought to behave in the household of God, which is the church of the living God, a pillar and buttress of the truth.* –1 Timothy 3:14-15

---

**3:14-16.** Paul hopes to visit Timothy in Ephesus, but the timing of his proposed visit is uncertain. Anticipating the possibility of a delay, he gives instructions concerning various aspects of the church. These verses reflect a second purpose of the letter. He charges Timothy with guiding the church, keeping in mind its importance in God's plan. The church is God's house (household), the church of the living God, pillar (*stulos*) and support (*hedraioma*) of the truth. These words are rich with meaning and set forth an exalted view of the church. They are worthy of additional study. Such word studies can be done easily using a concordance or Bible dictionary.

The chapter concludes with what may be an early Christian hymn that served as a profession of faith. Mystery is something previously hidden but now revealed. As noted earlier, mystery often refers to the inclusion of the Gentiles in the church, but the additional modifier "of godliness" suggests a different meaning here. (References to godliness occur frequently in the Pastoral Letters.) Godliness has to do with understanding the identity of Jesus.

Summarized briefly, the text speaks of Jesus' Incarnation, the coming and presence of the Spirit, the fulfillment of the angels' longing (1 Pet 1:12), the proclamation of the gospel, the faith response of human beings, and Jesus' ascension (or perhaps Second Coming). The parallelism is striking in the original text:

Who was revealed in flesh,
Was justified in spirit,
Was seen by angels,
Was proclaimed among the nations,
Was believed on the world,
Was taken up in glory.

These six truths summarize Jesus' life.

## The Message of the Chapter Summarized

"Let me share another faithful saying: when someone wants to serve as an overseer, he desires a good work. Select the right person as an overseer, considering his reputation, his marriage relationship, his personal character his abilities, his family, and his experience in the faith.

"In the same way, one who serves as a deacon must exhibit dignity and character. He must understand and accept God's plan to include everyone in the faith, having a clear conscience as he serves everyone equally. Let a man prove himself in these matters and then let him serve.

"In the same way, the women servants must exhibit dignity and character.

"A deacon must be the husband of one wife, managing his family well. Those who serve well gain a good level of dignity and confidence in the faith which is in Christ Jesus.

"I plan to come to you, but I may be delayed. With these instructions, you will know what to do in God's family, the church that supports and undergirds the truth. The truth is God's revelation about godliness. It all has to do with Jesus: he was seen in the flesh and vindicated in the spirit, seen by angels (heavenly beings) and proclaimed to every nation (earthly beings), believed on in the world and taken up to glory."

# 1 Timothy 4

*[Note: it is suggested that the student read the introductory materials in this guide before beginning an individual preparatory reading and analysis. It is important that the student learn to do this work for herself and not to depend only on the work and comments of others]*

## CONTENT
The outline and paragraphing included in the Content section of each chapter are only suggestions. The student is encouraged to identify the paragraphs and subsections within each paragraph in his own study. The paragraphing of the biblical text is fairly standard in modern translations.

To see where this chapter fits into the overall structure of the letter, refer to the outline in the Introduction. The first paragraph (4:1-5) is sometimes included with the purpose statement of 3:14-16.

Outline of the Chapter
| | |
|---|---|
| **4:1-5** | Prediction of a falling away and the presence of false teachers |
| **4:6-10** | How to be a good minister |
| **4:11-16** | Personal instructions for Timothy |

Observations about the Chapter
The teachings of this chapter are relatively straightforward and easily understood. The study helps for the chapter are brief since few explanations are needed to understand the message.

## STUDY HELPS
**4:1-5.** The later (or last) times may refer to a future time before the second coming of Jesus, but Chapter 1 and 4:7 suggest a present tense reality as well since the false teachers were already at work in Paul's day. The apostasy that is predicted has some ascetic elements. Various aspects of the false teaching are described: listening to deceiving spirits and teachings of demons

(perhaps in contrast to the reference to the words of the Spirit in v. 1), hypocritical liars with seared consciences, and false teachings about marriage and foods—teaching that it is necessary to abstain from both. God created all things good and has a good plan for his creation. The false teachings about marriage and foods reflect misunderstandings of God's original provision in the Garden. The point is that all creation is from God and is good, and that asceticism violates God's purpose.

**4:6-10.** Timothy is charged with correcting false teaching so that the church will not be misled (v. 6). The description of Timothy as a good "servant" (*diakonos*) uses the same word that is translated "deacon" in Chapter 3. Correct teaching provides nourishment by words of faith and good teaching. The word for teaching is also translated doctrine. "Good doctrine" here is similar to "sound (healthy) doctrine" in 1:10-11. Good doctrine avoids fables and myths (v. 7). A key to successful Christian living is self-discipline that focuses on godliness more than physical fitness. In the mention of physical fitness as secondary to godliness, one may see a reference to asceticism. Physical exercise and self-denial regarding physical things have value only in this life. Godliness has value both here and hereafter.

---

*Faithful is the word and worthy of full acceptance: for toward this we labor and strive, because we hope in the living God who is the Savior of all people, specifically of those who believe.* 1 Timothy 4:9-10

---

**4:9-10.** Here is the third "faithful saying": that the Christian mind is focused on God as the source of hope and salvation for all. This hope is worth striving for. Note the repeated reference to God as Savior.

**4:11-16.** Timothy is to teach and prescribe (*paraggello*) these things. Prescribe is a term used of strict military orders and suggests authority (cf. 1:3).

Timothy was a young man, a description that suggests he was less than 35 years of age, certainly less than 40. The false teachers would have pointed to such youth and inexperience as invalidating Timothy's teachings. Youth were not frequently placed in such positions of authority. Understanding the historical context is essential. Timothy is to be an example in various areas—speech, conduct, love, faith, and purity, all of which will allow him to demonstrate maturity. His example will reinforce his authority as he teaches these things and opposes false teaching.

**4:13.** Paul again mentions his plan to return to Ephesus (see 3:14) and urges upon Timothy in the meanwhile three things: public reading of Scripture, exhortation (preaching), and teaching.

**4:14-15.** Timothy was to develop his gift: be diligent in these things, be totally committed to them and absorbed by them, be a clear example to all. Nothing in the context suggests that the gift mentioned here was miraculous. Timothy had been given a gift related to teaching and ministry. The gift had been confirmed when the group of elders (*presbuteros*) placed their hands on him, and it was accompanied by prophetic words. (See comments at 2 Timothy 1:6-7 for a study of the New Testament practice of laying on hands.) Prophecy can mean prediction (foretelling), proclamation (forth-telling), or announcing the message of another (for-telling, speaking for another). In these verses, the second meaning best fits the context. The confirmation through proclamation may refer to the things said when Timothy received his gift, or it may refer to Timothy's abilities in teaching. The former seems more likely in the context.

Timothy's responsibility in ministry did not place him above other Christians. A part of his responsibility at Ephesus was teaching and preaching—actions that would bring salvation for him and his hearers. The verbs used in this section provide helpful understandings of the seriousness with which a Christian minister (and every Christian) should approach the Christian life and service: give attention (*prosecho*, be diligent, devote yourself), do not be neglectful (*ameleo*), take care of (*meletao*, revolve in the mind, meditate, practice), be (*eimi*, exist, be absorbed, be immersed), keep a close watch (*epecho*, hold yourself, persist).

## The Message of the Chapter Summarized

The primary purposes of this chapter are to help Timothy address the problems posed by the false teachers and to encourage him to develop himself as a good and faithful servant in his own study, teaching, and preaching.

"God through his Spirit has already made clear that the time is coming when some will depart from the faith with various deceits, demonic teachings, and insincerity because their consciences are no longer sensitive. They forbid marriage and the very foods that God created for us. God's creation is good. For us who believe and know the truth, God's creation is to be enjoyed with gratitude and recognized as holy through God's teachings and our grateful prayers.

"Timothy, you will be a good servant and you will show your training in faith and good teaching when you live according to God's words and teach others these things. Avoid silly fables and myths. Train yourself in godliness because it has value here and hereafter. Physical training is temporary, even as these teachings about abstinence only apply in this world. Here is the faithful word that summarizes this: we are diligent in these things because we hope in the living God who is Savior of all.

"In summary, command and teach these things. Avoid criticisms that focus on your youth—be an example in every aspect of life. Until I come, devote yourself to public reading of Scripture, teaching, and preaching. Develop your gift; it was given and confirmed by the elders. Do all of this continuously so that others can see how God develops godliness within us. Watch your life and watch your teachings so that God will work through you for your salvation and the salvation of those you teach."

# 1 Timothy 5

*[Note: it is suggested that the student read the introductory materials in this study guide before beginning any individual preparatory reading and analysis. The student should attempt to memorize the five steps of Bible study plan so that they become automatic. Remember that this guide is designed to assist you with your own study. Ideally, you should have your Bible open and at your side as you use this guide]*

## CONTENT

This reminder cannot be repeated too often: the paragraphing and descriptions included in this Content section are only a suggestion. The student is encouraged to identify the paragraphs and subsections within each paragraph in his or her own study. The division of the biblical text into paragraphs is fairly easy in this chapter and is generally the same in most contemporary translations.

Outline of the Chapter
While it is not always easy to discern how the historical setting of the book informs the message, the book of 1 Timothy must be read and understood against the background of the teachings and actions of the false teachers. Paul's desire was that the church function smoothly. The outline below is organized around the subjects and groups Paul mentions. This teaching section continues into Chapter 6.

| | |
|---|---|
| **5:1-2** | Healthy relationships with all members |
| **5:3-16** | Special instructions related to the widows |
| **5:17-25** | Special instructions related to the elders, plus some personal references |
| **6:1-2** | Matters related to slaves |
| **6:3-10** | Matters related to false teachers |

*[The last two points are included for completeness and parallelism in the outline, but will be treated in the Study Helps for Chapter 6.]*

## STUDY HELPS

**5:1-2.** Timothy is to establish healthy relationships with all members of the local church. Older men, older women, younger men, and younger women are mentioned. The word elder or older man (*presbuteros*) is used with two meanings in the context of 1 Timothy 5: one with reference to a church leader (4:14; 5:17), the other referring to an older man (v. 1, cf. Tit. 2:1).

Note the close connections and the parallels between Chapter 3 and Chapter 5. The elders of 5:17 are apparently the same group as the overseers of 3:1, also mentioned in 4:14; the widows of 5:9 are likely the same group as the women in 3:11 (see my comments on Chapter 3, especially 3:11). Timothy is to treat the older men as fathers, the older women as mothers, the younger men as brothers, and the younger women as sisters with purity. The phrase "with purity" perhaps applies to every group, but this instruction would be especially important in Timothy's relationship with the young women in the church.

**5:3-8.** The word "honor," both in v. 3 and v. 17, may denote a salary given by the church. This seems the best understanding in the context. Perhaps the church provided monetary help for needy widows, for widows who were servant helpers, and for certain elders.

The family of a widow had the first obligation to provide care and support. Some widows were neglected by their own families. Both children and grandchildren are mentioned as those who have responsibility in this matter. The responsibility must be accepted in order to please God. The church has always cared for its members.

**5:5-6.** The one who is truly a widow is all alone (without any family) and depends on God. Her dependence on God is evident in her prayers. The exact meaning of v. 6 is hard to determine—some think it suggests that some widows were forced to turn to prostitution. It may mean that they were especially susceptible to exploitation by the false teachers (cf. 2 Tim. 3:6). Self-indulgence (*spatalao*, live in pleasure or wantonness) is never the lifestyle that characterizes Christians.

**5:7-8.** Timothy was to carefully teach these things so all would know and could be above reproach with regard to such obligations. The Jews had invented various ways to avoid the obligation of children to help their parents (Mark 7), but Christians joyfully accept the opportunity and obligation to care for those of their family. To do otherwise is to act as an unbeliever.

The grammatical construction of v. 8 demands consideration. "If anyone does not provide for his relatives…." Literally, the text reads "of his own and especially of his own house." The pronoun is plural. A Christian with needy relatives is obligated to care for them or he becomes worse than an unbeliever and is denying the faith. Consider what happens if one reads the text too literally. "I do not have 'relatives,' I have only one needy person in my family and so I am not obligated. After all, Paul said 'relatives,'' not 'relative.'" What absurdity! The only way to communicate the point Paul is making is to use the plural form to cover every number, whether one, two, or more. Every Christian is obligated by this verse, regardless of the specific number of relatives. The verse clearly applies to those with only one widow in the family.

The construction is significant because of the parallel construction that mentions the "children" of overseers (3:4). Some have argued that an overseer must have two or more children, based on the use of the word children in 3:4. But in parallel to 5:8, the construction that Paul uses is a customary way of saying one, two, or more. (See also the same kind of construction in 5:16.)

**5:9-16.** Some widows were put on a roll, perhaps a list of designated female servants (again, see my comments on 3:11). The widows included on the roll were to be at least 60 years old and were to have been the wife of one man, with a reputation for good works. Five specific good deeds are listed. It appears that widows on the list would have been described by all of these five actions: having raised children, showing hospitality, having washed feet, having cared for the afflicted, and having been devoted to every good work.

**5:11-12.** Some widows, younger widows, were not to be put on the list. The context indicates that those on the list had committed themselves to service in the church and had made the decision not to remarry. This text does not disparage marriage (or remarriage) for widows; this text encourages a healthy practice of God's plan for marriage. Younger widows might be tempted to make the commitment to service in the church and afterward want to marry. In this context, the problem is not remarriage, but making a vow and not keeping it. The problem is not that passions move us away from Christ; the problem is making a vow to Christ and then abandoning it.

**5.13.** In light of v. 14, this passage appears to continue the reference to the younger widows. The younger widows as they worked in daily ministry, care, and food distribution would interact with many persons. With the energy of youth, they might find it difficult to have enough to do to fill their days. Paul writes that such a life could present a temptation to idleness, gossiping and being busybodies. Therefore, he urges the younger widows to remarry, bear children, keep house, and live above criticism.

**5:15.** Perhaps Timothy had communicated to Paul specific examples of the problems mentioned in v. 6 and v. 13. It is possible to understand vv. 15-16 as a unit, so that those who have turned aside to follow Satan (in materialism) are those described in v. 16. Regardless of the difficult interpretive questions in this passage, Christian families must fulfill their responsibility to older family members. The church will thus be able to help those who are truly widows—those without any family on which they can depend.

**5:16.** It is interesting that the best Greek texts limit the instructions of this verse to Christian women. In the previous verses, the application was made to Christian families. Are there points of connection by which these concluding verses would inform the instructions concerning the younger widows (the most obvious antecedent), or the instructions about widows generally? Additional questions to be studied always arise in the careful analysis of the biblical text.

The construction of 5:16 is parallel to 5:8, giving another good example of the plural pronoun being used to cover every situation. The obligation to the family was clear, even if a believing sister had only one relative who was a widow.

**5:17-22.** The use of the word "elder" here seems to refer back to the overseers (3:1), on the basis of the verbs "rule, preach, and teach." While ruling could refer only to households, the context suggests that the service and activity of these leaders had to do with the entire church. "Honor" can refer to esteem or to salary; the context suggests the latter. The citation from the Old Testament is from Deut. 25:4. That some elders were working in teaching and preaching suggests that others were not. Not all leaders have the same gifts or talents. The use of the term elders in the New Testament is always plural, but what the actual practice might have been in a city with multiple house churches is unclear. For example, were there elders in each local house church, parallel to the elders in each family in Israel, so that the elders from the various local assemblies made up the eldership in that city? The church in the first century did not have the kind of institutional organizational challenges that churches face today in our capitalistic, enterprise-oriented context where the elders often function more as administrators than as shepherds.

**5:19.** The verb in this verse (present, middle, imperative, *paradechomai*, to accept or to admit) can suggest an action in process, which with the negative particle indicates an action to be stopped rather than an action to be continued. This admonition may address the difficulties that were arising from within the eldership, or it may reflect some of the problems and accusations that were arising from the presence of the false teachers. The concept of requiring two or three witnesses is taught in the Old Testament (Deut. 17:6) and was the standard in every case, not just in the case of leaders.

**5:20.** This verse seems to refer also to the leaders. Those who continue in sin must be called out or challenged, and this must be done "in the presence of all" so others will not practice sin. "In the presence of all" could refer to the churches or to the other elders. The Bible gives instructions about how to deal with sin. An often-repeated observation is that the rebuke should be as public as the knowledge of the sin. (For parallels and related texts, see Rom. 16:17-18; 1 Cor. 5; Gal. 6:1-5; 1 Thess. 5:4; 2 Thess. 3:6-15; Tit. 3:10-11).

**5.21.** The admonition of this verse repeats the charge to Timothy—that he should hold fast or guard the principles without partiality, applying the teachings equally to all. While the principle clearly applies to Timothy's relationship with all people, the context suggests that this verse should be understood as a continuation of the instructions about the elders.

**5:22.** This verse has three imperatives: do not lay hands too quickly; do not share the sins of others; keep yourself free from sin. In the context, the most obvious application has to do with naming and restoring elders. The wisdom of and reason for encouraging hesitation in the selection of leaders could be to identify correctly the false teachers. Some of the false teachers may have arisen from within the eldership. The idea of "sharing responsibility for the sins of others" suggests that too rapid affirmation could be seen as approval of the actions of others. Keep yourself pure likely refers to the context of church leadership and not to general purity of life (5:23).

**5:23.** This verse seems to be parenthetical, an explanation that purity (mentioned in v. 22) does not demand abstinence from wine since Timothy must manage his stomach problems and illnesses. The culture of that day accepted wine drinking—whether added to water for purification, or as a beverage. In the case of leaders, the Bible warns against drunkenness or much wine (3:3; Tit. 1:7). In 3:13, the inappropriate use of wine may be associated with violence and quarreling.

Every effort to understand what the Bible says must take into account the context. Without considering the context, the text may be misread and the message misunderstood and misapplied. Every Bible student must be careful not to make the text say what it did not specifically say in the original context. On the other hand, the principles that are set forth in Scripture must be understood and applied as we live as Christians in the culture, society, and world we know today.

**5:24-25.** These verses resume the topic of 5:17-22 and are probably directly related to v. 22. False teaching is obvious by content and consequences. Nonetheless, some things related to the false teachers will remain hidden until judgment.

# The Message of the Chapter Summarized

Knowing how to act in the church involves understanding interpersonal relationships and holding people accountable for their actions. Nowhere is this more important than in church matters that have to do with money. When a group of widows receives money, the number of applicants to the group is large. Some widows who have families that could help them are tempted by money; some of the families would like to transfer the care of their mother or grandmother to the church. Younger widows may look at the money to be received before they consider what kind of life they will want in the future. When church leaders or elders receive money from the church, one can anticipate more volunteers. A man who genuinely wants to serve as an overseer seeks the good of God's people before his own good. When money enters the picture, numerous problems can arise.

Paul's instructions to Timothy can be summarized like this: be careful!

"Develop good interpersonal relationships with all of the members.

"Widows who are genuinely widows depend on God and can be enrolled in the list of servants, but be careful because family members have the first obligation to care for their own. Those who are enrolled are examples of service. Do not enroll widows who do not meet the age requirement. Not only will younger widows face various personal challenges, they may experience other problems. It is best that they marry and manage their children and households. Again, believers must take care of their own widows so the church is not burdened to the point that it cannot take care of those who genuinely need help.

"Elders are worthy of honor—both in appreciation and in money. Laborers deserve wages and oxen are allowed to eat the grain as they work. Carefully check every charge brought against an elder. When sin is present, make the rebuke public. Do not prejudge any case and do not show partiality. Be careful about giving your blessing too quickly, or you can easily appear to be siding with wrong. Keep yourself pure. (I am talking about elders and your work with them. This does not mean you should not keep using a little wine to help with your stomach problems and your frequent illnesses.)

"Some of the sins you have to deal with will be obvious, others may remain unknown or may appear later. What I will tell you is that good works are always obvious and that they cannot be hidden."

# 1 Timothy 6

*[Note: it is suggested that the student read the introductory materials in this guide before beginning an individual preparatory reading and analysis of this chapter.]*

## CONTENT

The paragraphing included in the Content section of each chapter gives suggestions concerning how the thoughts in the chapter are organized and how they can be grouped for outlining. The student is encouraged to identify the paragraphs and subsections within each paragraph based on her or his own reading and study. The student will be well-served to try to summarize the contents of each paragraph and develop her or his own paragraph headings.

Outline of the Chapter
**6:1-2**      About slaves
**6:3-10**     About the false teachers, false teachings, and true riches
*Note: The first two sections seem to continue from Chapter 5 the instructions concerning the treatment of various groups in the church; see the outline at the beginning of Chapter 5 and the observations below.*
**6:11-16**    Personal instructions to Timothy
**6:17-19**    About rich Christians
**6:20-21**    Conclusion

Observations about the Chapter
        The instructions in the first two sections of this chapter (6:1-2; 6:3-10) seem to be closely related to the instructions about various groups that began in 5:1. Paul instructs Timothy about the older men, older women, younger men, and younger women, with extended instructions concerning widows, and elders. The first two sections in Chapter 6 add instructions about slaves and false teachers, although 6:3-10 may be better

understood as part of the conclusion of the letter (see comments below on 6:3-10).

## STUDY HELPS

**6:1-2.** If the instructions of this section seem out of context, remember that instructions to slaves often followed similar instructions to other groups, either in the context of the family or the context of the church (Eph. 5-6; Col. 3-4; Tit. 2). These verses may reflect and seek to counteract the teachings of the false teachers about slaves and slavery.

Christian slaves honor their masters, and in so doing they also honor God. Christians slaves who are blessed with Christians masters must serve well because they are serving brothers in Christ.

Paul urges Timothy to teach and preach (*parakaleo*, exhort, encourage) these truths.

**6:3-10.** As he moves toward a conclusion of the book, Paul returns to the subject of 1:3-11. This was a common practice in concluding a letter. The false teachers were those who opposed or contradicted Paul's teachings. Therefore, their doctrines were (1) false and different, (2) did not agree with sound (healthy) words, and (3) did not lead to godliness. Some of the characteristics of the teachings of the false teachers are repeated in these verses. The false teachers were conceited, without understanding, and lovers of controversy and arguments about words. Wherever the false teachers were present, envy, dissension, slander, suspicions, and conflicts were also present. They were seeking to benefit financially from their false teaching (cf. Tit. 1:9-11).

**6:6-10.** The value of godliness is clear when it is accompanied by contentment—without pride and without self-sufficiency. The things of this world are only for this world. The riches of this world are temporal and a source of temptation, leading many into temptation and away from the faith to grief and destruction.

For Christians, it is enough to have basic necessities and a contented spirit. The focus on money (possibly a reference to the concept of "honor" in 5:3 and 5:17) leads to evil and all kinds of problems.

**6:11-16**. The conclusion of the book is near. The instructions in these verses are specifically directed to Timothy. "Flee from these things" probably refers to the things mentioned in vv. 3-10. Note the four verbs: flee, pursue, fight, take hold. Timothy is admonished to flee (*pheugo*); he is told to pursue (*dioko*) six things—righteousness, godliness, faith, love, perseverance, gentleness. He is admonished to fight (*agonizomai*) the good fight and to take hold (*epilambanomai*) of eternal life, consistent with his calling and confession.

      **6:13-16.** These verses are one sentence in Greek; the charge (*paraggello* is the verb form) given to Timothy here is reminiscent of the charge with which the book begins (cf. 1:3). The doxology of v. 15-16 may reflect an early Christian hymn.

> *His appearing in its own time will reveal…*
> *The blessed and only Sovereign*
> *The King of kings*
> *The Lord of lords*
> *Who alone has immortality*
> *Living in unapproachable light*
> *Whom no human has seen or can see*
> *To whom is honor and eternal might.*

**6:17-19.** "As for the rich…." These verses are also one sentence in Greek. It is possible to see these verses as a separate paragraph dealing with another subgroup in the church, "the rich." The reference to riches reminds one of 6:6-10. Perhaps "the rich" represents a final group about which Paul gives instructions, given the parallel construction in Chapters 5-6. Regardless, Timothy is to instruct them (*paraggello*) not to be proud, not to set their hope on uncertain riches, to keep on doing good, to be rich in good deeds, to be generous, and to share. By so doing, they are storing up and preparing for the future and genuine life. In the context of many Western societies, these instructions provide a helpful guide to the Christian life, given that we are rich in this world's goods in comparison to the rest of the world.

**6:20-21.** "O Timothy" is parallel to "O man of God" (6:11). In the closing admonition, Timothy is to guard the treasure entrusted to him and to avoid the false teachings and false knowledge that move one away from faith rather than closer to it. In the phrase "grace to you" the pronoun is plural, even though the letter is addressed to and named for an individual. This construction likely indicates that the letter was to be read and shared with the church. Plural endings are part of all of the Pastoral Letters (2 Tim. 4:22; Tit. 3:15).

## The Message of the Chapter Summarized

"Slaves should honor their masters because in this way they also honor God and his teaching. Slaves with believing masters are honored to serve those who are their brothers.

"Here is what you must teach. I am thinking again about the false teachers. They have different doctrines, they contradict the words of Jesus and the teaching that leads to godliness. They are conceited and without understanding. They love arguments; problems follow them. Therefore, you must make clear that godliness leads to contentment regarding the things of this world. The possessions of this world are only for this world. We can be content as long as we have what we need. Desires bring temptations, traps, and troubles.

"Flee these things; pursue righteousness, godliness, faith, love, perseverance, and kindness. Take hold of eternal life. I charge you to live above reproach as you anticipate Jesus' coming. What a day of blessing, glory, and praise that will be! Just think of what it means that he is King of Kings and Lord of Lords!

"The rich must not hope in riches but in God. It is enough to do good, be rich in good works, and be generous in sharing. This leads to real treasure and real life.

"I charge you, Timothy, guard these words that I have given you, avoid the false knowledge that the false teachers 'babble forth.' You know it leads away from faith. May God's grace be with you all."

# 2 Timothy 1

*[Note: it is suggested that the student read the introductory materials in this guide before beginning an individual preparatory reading and analysis.]*

## CONTENT

The paragraphing included in the Content section of each chapter is merely a suggestion or guide. The student is encouraged to identify the paragraphs and subsections within each paragraph in his or her own reading, analysis, and study.

Often the division of the text into paragraphs is fairly standard in modern translations. In this chapter, however, some disagreement about the division of this chapter exists. I have divided the longer section of 1:3-14 into two shorter paragraphs, even though linguistically it should likely be considered a single paragraph, in part due to the fact that 1:8-14 is one long sentence in Greek.

Outline of the Chapter

| | |
|---|---|
| **1:1-2** | Greeting or salutation |
| **1:3-7** | The faith and heritage of Timothy |
| **1:8-14** | Be loyal to the gospel—not ashamed, willing to suffer, guarding healthy teaching |
| **1:15-18** | Update on Paul's situation |

## STUDY HELPS

**1:1-2.** The salutation mentions the writer (Paul, apostle) and the recipient (Timothy, dear son). As in the first letter, Paul's description of himself as an apostle emphasizes his authority. His desire to establish his apostolic authority is understandable in view of the fact that the letter was to be read to the church. That Paul was writing to combat false teaching may explain the need for identifying Paul as one with apostolic authority.

That Timothy is described as a son to Paul reflects a close relationship similar to that of father and son. The Bible does not say that Paul baptized Timothy (compare 1:18; see also Acts 16 where Timothy was apparently already a Christian when Paul met him). The close association of Paul and Timothy serves to give Timothy authority.

Paul writes to instruct Timothy about false teachers (as in the first letter). Paul, anticipating his death, seeks to give Timothy the authority needed to address the problems arising from the false teachings.

Paul's mention of the promise of life in Christ Jesus may arise from the fact that he is writing near the end of his life, anticipating his death (see 4:1-8).

**1:3-7.** Including a word of thanksgiving to God was a customary part of the Greek letter form used in the New Testament. Paul's mention of his prayers for Timothy is parallel to his prayers for the churches to which he was writing (e.g., 1 Thess. 1:1-2). In this paragraph (1:3-7), Paul urges Timothy to remember his life, family, and calling. Remembering these things was an encouragement to Paul. To remember this spiritual history would also be a source of spiritual strength and encouragement to Timothy. Timothy was blessed by a spiritual heritage that he had received from his grandmother and mother. This memory would strengthen Timothy's desire to correct false teaching.

**1:5.** "Sincere" is literally unhypocritical (*anupokritos*, without pretense), perhaps foreshadowing the idea that the false teachers were not sincere and were pretentious.

**1:6-7.** Timothy had been well prepared for the task Paul gives him. (Timothy's preparation and giftedness are also mentioned in 1 Tim. 1:18 and 4:14.) Here the text describes the gift as received "through" or "by" Paul's hands. In 1 Tim. 4:14, a different preposition is used — "with" the hands of the elders. Parallel passages from the New Testament suggest that "laying on hands" refers to blessing and commissioning more often than imparting gifts or official status. Laying on hands in Acts 6:6 is accompanied with prayer for the purpose of appointing the Seven as special servants or ministers. Acts 1:26 does not mention laying on hands in the appointment of Matthias as an apostle to take Judas' place. Acts 8:17 describes laying on hands in a special circumstance to give God's blessing (through the apostles) to the opening of the gospel to the Samaritans. Such a variety of contexts and applications makes clear that one should not understand laying on hands to indicate apostolic succession.

The word gift (*charisma*) is singular. It often refers to a spiritual endowment or qualification. The New Testament does not give details about a time or times when Paul appointed Timothy by laying on hands. The reference to what God gives in v. 7 suggests a possible connection between v. 6 and v. 7. If so, v. 7 is a description of the gift. Since v. 7 can apply to all Christians ("to us"), it is possible in v. 6 that Paul is encouraging Timothy by reminding him of how God works in the lives of Christians.

**1:7.** "Spirit" can refer to the Holy Spirit (Spirit) or to one's attitude and desire (spirit). The Greek word for spirit has no definite article in this verse. In either understanding, the Christian is not timid, but has a (S)spirit of power, love, and self-discipline. Again, this verse does not apply exclusively to Timothy; it can be applied to Christians generally. Timothy has been prepared and empowered for God's purpose in his life.

**1:8-14.** These verses are one extended sentence in Greek, which I have treated as a single paragraph in these notes. The Greek construction can be seen as support for the idea that the paragraph is 1:3-14, and not just the one sentence of vv. 8-14.

**1:8-10.** Ashamed appears three times in the passage (vv. 8, 12, 16). Timothy is to testify without being ashamed of the gospel or of Paul. The "testimony of our Lord" is either the witness of Jesus or the witness about Jesus. The gospel is God's calling to holiness. In the gospel is revealed God's power; in the gospel God's grace and purpose are seen, revealed in Christ's coming to destroy death by bringing light and immortality. Timothy is called upon to suffer (*sugkakopatheo*, suffer evil together) for the gospel. The mention of suffering (1:8) surfaces several times throughout the book of 2 Timothy.

God's salvation and holy calling are not according to (*kata*) human works of merit, but according to God's purpose and grace which God planned and gave in Christ Jesus before time eternal. This salvation has now been revealed by the appearing (*epiphaneia*, compare our word epiphany) of our Savior Jesus Christ. In the Pastoral Letters, God is described as Savior and Jesus is described as Savior. Both were instrumental in our salvation. The sentence continues with two dependent participles: "having destroyed death" and "having made visible life and immorality." Both of these Jesus did through the gospel!

**1:11-14.** Paul describes himself as herald, apostle, and teacher for the gospel. "Appointed" (*tithemi*) reflects God's part in Paul's calling. A herald (*kerux*) is one who announces or proclaims (*kerusso*) the message (*kerygma*) of another. *Kerygma* is used in the New Testament to describe apostolic preaching. Since herald is today a little used word and has a special meaning, a good translation into contemporary English is preacher. (A study of fifteen Greek words that are translated as "preach" in the New Testament is available on my website: http://www.bobyoungresources.com/bible/grkprch.htm.) Apostle is repeated from 1:1 and carries the idea of having authority as one sent to represent another.

If the phrase "to the Gentiles" is accepted as authentic, a primary reason for Paul's sufferings is his efforts to take the gospel to the Gentiles. Paul was confident of his calling and confident of God's ability to protect him. He seeks to transfer this attitude to Timothy.

**1:12.** How should the words "my deposit" (NIV, what I have entrusted to him) be understood? Is the deposit something God has given to Paul (as in v. 14 with reference to Timothy) or something Paul has given to God? One can translate "trust," since a deposit is entrusted to another. The Greek uses the genitive/ablative form (of me or from me, my deposit) which opens the possibility of meanings other than the possessive. Either Paul has entrusted something to God and is confident that God will guard it, or Paul is convinced that God will protect the purity of the gospel described in vv. 8-10, the deposit of the gospel which God has entrusted to Paul. Another option is to see that Paul has entrusted his life and destiny to God. These options hinge on how one translates the Greek words "my deposit" or "my trust." The use of "deposit" in v. 14 is less difficult because it is not modified with the personal pronoun; the literal reading is "the good deposit" (see comments immediately below).

**1:13-14.** Sound words means healthy teaching. The Greek word that is translated "sound" (*hugiaino*) has the same root as our word hygiene. Timothy is to be guided by what he has heard from Paul. "To keep" or "to have" the healthy teaching means holding fast rather than observing or obeying. Timothy is to hold fast to the type or pattern (*hupotuposis*) Paul has given him. Timothy is to guard (same verb as v. 12) the good deposit (same word as v. 12). In the context, the reference in v. 14 is most certainly to the gospel. Reading the same meaning for the word in v. 12 gives this sense: "I am convinced that he is able to guard my gospel until that day." However, the use of the same words (guard, deposit) with two different meanings in the same context could also be a literary device. Finally, despite the repetition of both the noun and the verb, I conclude that v. 14 does not necessarily help with understanding the meaning of v. 12.

Healthy teaching comes from God. The false teachers cannot claim that their teaching is from God. The teaching Paul brought and passed on to Timothy was from God, and was therefore authoritative. The affirmation that the Holy Spirit dwells in Timothy should be noted. Timothy will be helped in his work by God's very presence. Much of the contents of this introductory section of the letter points to the fact that one of Paul's reasons for writing was to identify and oppose false teachers.

**1:15-18.** "Everyone in Asia" is obviously exaggeration; the phrase is hyperbole. The meaning is that many have deserted Paul, including two who are unknown to us elsewhere in Scripture, named only here. Verses 16-18 use the Greek optative mood, in this case indicating a prayerful desire of Paul. Onesiphorus is mentioned again in 4:19. We do not have details elsewhere of the events mentioned by Paul in this text.

### The Message of the Chapter Summarized

"Paul, an apostle, to Timothy my child: grace and peace.

"When I think about and pray about the time we have shared, I long to see you. I remember the faith of your grandmother and mother, a faith that is now in you. It is time to renew your spiritual fire and use your gift. Since God did not give us a spirit of fear, it is time to show power, love, and self-control. That means not being ashamed of the gospel and being willing to share whatever suffering is necessary for the gospel. Through the gospel, God saved us and called us, according to his purpose and grace that are now made known in Jesus as he broke death's hold and revealed life and immortality.

"What a privilege to serve this gospel, as preacher, apostle, and teacher, even though it means suffering. I am not ashamed because I know in whom I have faith and he will protect what he entrusted to me.

"Hold the pattern of healthy teaching that you heard from me, protect what has been entrusted to you with the power of the Holy Spirit living in you.

"Those in Asia have deserted me, I am grateful for Onesiphorus who has ministered to my needs here in Rome, even as he did in Ephesus."

# 2 Timothy 2

*[Note: it is suggested that the student read the introductory materials in this guide before beginning an individual preparatory reading and analysis.]*

## CONTENT

The paragraphing, outlining, and descriptions included in the Content section of each chapter are only suggestions or guides. The student is encouraged to identify the paragraphs and subsections within each paragraph in his or her own study, and to think about how she or he would summarize the contents of the paragraph. In most chapters of the Bible, the division of the biblical text into paragraphs is fairly standardized in modern translations.

Outline of the Chapter

**2:1-13**      Endure hardships (continuation of thoughts from the sentence in 1:8-14)

**2:14-26**      How to handle controversies

*Notes: The chapter naturally divides itself into two major paragraphs. It may be helpful to identify smaller units of the text due to the length of the major paragraphs.*

*Homiletic paragraphing (how the text divides itself for sermonic applications) may focus on the illustrations Paul uses to describe the Christian worker.*

## STUDY HELPS

**2:1-13.** Paul repeats the description of Timothy as his child (cf. 1 Tim. 1:2, 2 Tim. 1:1). "Be strong" applies to the instructions Paul is giving Timothy, continuing the instructions of 1:8-14. This verb (be strong) may also connect to 1:15 in the sense that those who did not remain with Paul were not strong. Strength is required to endure suffering and hardship. As Timothy has been entrusted with what he heard from Paul (1:13-14), he is to continue the process for future generations. Four generations are in view in 2:1-2: Paul, Timothy, faithful men, and others. Entrust (*paratithemi*) is a verb from the same Greek root as the noun form "deposit" in 1:12 and 1:14.

**2:3-6**. Paul sets forth several examples to encourage Timothy and to teach endurance: soldiers, athletes, and farmers. Likely, all of the examples are to be related to suffering in some way (v. 3).

**2:7.** Some have seen here a reference to the Holy Spirit since one of the ways God gives insight is through the teachings of the Holy Spirit. Such is not demanded by the text, even though the suggestion provides an interesting connection between 1:7, 1:14, and 2:7. The student interested in understanding the message of Scripture must take care not to read with preconceived ideas. This verse contains no internal justification for attributing the understanding mentioned here to the Holy Spirit.

**2:8-13.** This section is based not in illustrations from common human experience, but in various truths about Jesus, Paul, and the gospel. The use of the word "remember" parallels 1:3-6. The focus is on suffering hardships. The reference to Jesus' resurrection should be understood as including his suffering. Paul is suffering in prison, chained as a criminal would be (cf. 1:8, 2:3). Paul is anticipating his death (4:1-7). Paul endures because he has the salvation of God's chosen people in mind. He is willing to do whatever is necessary to advance the gospel. Even though Paul is chained, the gospel is not chained! In Phil. 1:12-14, Paul explains how on another occasion his imprisonment was advancing the gospel.

"My gospel" is interesting in light of "my deposit" in 1:12. Paul is not the source or the subject of the gospel. The gospel has been entrusted to him. Because he serves as a herald or preacher, it is his message, even though it was received from another. This gospel (word of God) continues to go forth freely even when the messengers suffer and are imprisoned.

The conclusion of the paragraph makes clear that Paul's motive for suffering is the salvation of God's chosen ones. Paul affirms this goal as motivation for his suffering; it was obviously the reason for Christ's suffering.

**2:11-13.** Here is the fourth of the five "faithful sayings" in the Pastoral Letters. Each of these sayings reflects an important biblical truth. The saying cited here was perhaps an early creedal statement or hymn. The first class conditional statements assume the truthfulness of each statement; these are not conditional possibilities. I have attempted to reflect this grammatical construction in the translation immediately below. The first two verbs are positive (what it means to endure hardship); the second two verbs are negative ideas (describing lack of endurance).

---

*Faithful is this message: Because we died together, we will live together; because we endure, we will reign together; when we deny, he will also deny us; when we are unfaithful, he remains faithful, for he cannot deny himself.* 2 Tim. 2:11-13

---

**2:14-26.** The word "remember" reflects a common, repeated theme in the book. "These things" can either look back to 2:1-13, or forward to 2:14-26. In the context, my preference is the latter. Ashamed in v. 15 is repeated from earlier references in the letter.

**2:14-19.** This section is characterized by several words and phrases related to "speaking:" remind, testify, quarreling about words, ruining listeners, word of truth, godless chatter, false teaching, truth, God's solid foundation (word), and confessing the name of the Lord. The result of much talking is more and more ungodliness.

Timothy is to confront both the negative actions and the false teachings. To do so, he must be diligent (*spoudazo*, be eager, do your best). He must be God's worker (*paristemi*, present yourself, v. 15), wholly depending on God and God's word. One who faithfully fulfills these duties will be approved. Some have seen in the verb "handling correctly" (*orthotomeo*, literally, cutting straight) a reference related to Paul's work in tent making.

Notice Paul's statement that false teachings spread like gangrene. The saying is true: bad news travels fast! Two false teachers are mentioned by name: Hymenaeus (cf. 1 Tim. 1:20) and Philetus (not mentioned elsewhere in the Bible). The text identifies the false teaching as a misunderstanding about the resurrection, specifically the belief that it is already past. This misunderstanding likely refers to the belief that Jesus had already returned. The New Testament mentions in other places some misunderstandings of the Day of the Lord, the second coming, and the resurrection (cf. 2 Thess. 2:1-3; 1 Cor. 15, et.al.).

Some of our knowledge of the misunderstandings and false teachings that were present in the churches in the first century comes from historical information. Those details inform our understanding of the Bible. Bringing together the Bible and first century historical data, one can see the influences of Judaism, Greek philosophy, asceticism, and Gnosticism in the religious climate of the first century. Understanding these influences helps us analyze the nature of the false teachings. With regard to the misunderstandings of the resurrection, a short list of factors from the first century context would include the influence of dualism and Greek philosophy, the idea that the resurrection the Bible describes is the new spiritual life (e.g. Romans 6) and is not related to the physical body, Gnosticism, the belief of the Sadducees that there was no resurrection, and teachings like those described in 2 Thess. 2.

**2:19.** "Foundation" is a common metaphor in Paul's writings. In this verse, it is likely a reference to the Scriptures (Old Testament) with the biblical citation possibly based on Num. 16:5. 1 Tim. 3:15 describes the church as upholding the truth. The word of God is certain (sealed), and cannot be destroyed by false teaching (see also 3:9). The second quotation in this verse is from an unknown source. The teaching of this paragraph (2:14-19) is that it is necessary to oppose false teaching and that God has provided the resources in his word to combat the false teachers.

**2:20-26.** In this paragraph is an illustration about different kinds of equipment (vessels) with different purposes. In human experience in the everyday world, some vessels, although important, have ignoble uses (compare 1 Cor. 12:22-24). The reference may be to vessels used for carrying excrement—vessels that were extremely important but had a less than noble use. The goal of every Christian is to fulfill God's noblest purposes—to be set apart, useful, and ready for God's work. The Christian life requires cleansing (*ekkathairo*, related to our word catharsis, possibly a reference to putting aside the false teachings and the accompanying actions). The cleansing "from these" refers to the useless words, false teaching, and misleading beliefs of 2:14-19.

**2:22-26.** These instructions to Timothy are reminiscent of 1 Tim. 4:11-12 and 6:11-14. The point is clear in v. 23: have nothing to do with the arguments and quarrels, teach with gentleness while enduring evil. The specific context in which the teaching mentioned in v. 24 is to be applied is made clear in v. 25. Those who have been led astray by the false teachers are to be corrected. Those who accept the false teachings will vehemently oppose the truth, but the correct approach is gentle instruction and godly hope that they will come to know truth and turn back from the influences of the false teachers. These influences are described here as a trap of the devil that captures people so that they do his will rather than God's will. The idea of being influenced to do the devil's will is the most likely reading, although the grammatical construction will allow an alternate reading: "escape the devil's trap to do God's will."

## The Message of the Chapter Summarized

"Timothy, my child, be strong. I want you to entrust the gospel to faithful men who will teach others to teach others. Be willing to suffer as a soldier of Jesus Christ so you please your commander. Run the race according to God's instructions. Work hard and you will be rewarded. I know you can understand what I am saying.

"Remember that Jesus Christ suffered and was raised from the dead. I suffer in prison for the salvation of God's chosen ones. The saying is sure: because we died with him, we will live with him; because we endure, we will reign with him; when we renounce, he will renounce us; when we are without faith, he is always faithful.

"Remind the church not to get into word battles that only serve to raise questions about faith. Be diligent to present yourself to God as a proven worker without shame, teaching the message accurately. Godless chatter leads to ungodliness and this message grows incredibly rapidly, as it has with two whom you know. They have left the truth when they say the resurrection has already occurred. What they believe will not change

God's sure word, and God knows those who are his—those who confess with their mouth and turn from evil in their lives.

"In a house are many different utensils, some for less noble uses. To be an honorable vessel for God it is necessary to be clean from the things of the world and to pursue the things of God. Reject word fights, because the Lord's servant teaches with kindness, patience and gentleness, hoping that God will change the minds of those who have strayed so they can escape the trap of the devil that has ensnared them."

# 2 Timothy 3

*[Note: it is suggested that the student reread the introductory materials in this guide before beginning an individual preparatory reading and analysis. The Bible study steps outlined there should become second nature as the student approaches a new section of Scripture.]*

## CONTENT
The paragraphing included in the Content section of each chapter is merely a suggestion or guide. The student is encouraged to identify the paragraphs and subsections within each paragraph as part of his or her own study. The division of this short chapter into paragraphs is fairly standard in modern translations.

Outline of the Chapter
**3:1-9**      Ungodliness in the last days
**3:10-17**    Paul instructs Timothy about persecution and the importance of persevering in God's Word

## STUDY HELPS
**3:1-9.** "Last days" is perhaps parallel to 1 Tim. 4:1. Note however that here the text reads "last days" (*eschatais hemerais*) while in 1 Tim. 4:1 it reads in "later times" (*husterois kairois*). The reference in both texts seems to be to a future time, although it also seems the situation described is already present or at least in development. The false teaching described in the context of these verses is already present.

      **3:1-5.** In the last days, terrible (difficult) times will come. "Times" is the same word as is used in 1 Tim. 4:1. The actions of godless people are described. These people may appear to be godly (they have a form of godliness, v. 5) but because of their manner of life, God and their version of godliness have no power to change them. In the context, this description probably refers to the false teachers and those influenced by the false teachers. They are to be avoided.

      **3:6-9.** It is difficult to fill in the details behind these verses because we have no parallel New Testament references to help us understand them. The description of "unstable women" (3:6) may remind one of certain women who were influenced by false teachers in 1 Timothy 5. In this text (3:6-9), we understand that in Ephesus certain women were described as guilt-ridden, without strong wills, filled with desires, and victimized by the false teachers. The gender of the Greek words shows that v. 7 also refers to the women; they are constantly learning but never able to gain a full knowledge (*epignosis*) of truth (anarthrous, without the article). Secular writers from the period noted that Gnosticism especially sought to influence women. The reference may be to the false teachers already described, to other false teachers with roots in Gnosticism, or a combination of the two.

These teachers stealthily enter houses and take captive (the minds of?) such women. "Take captive" likely refers to influencing their thinking (see NIV translation, gain control). Paul writes to warn Timothy (and the church) of these things.

**3:8-9.** To make clear the danger involved, Paul gives the example of Jannes and Jambres. In Jewish tradition, these are the names of the Egyptian court magicians who opposed Moses (Exod. 7:11). In the same way, the false teachers oppose truth. The false teachers are beyond hope—corrupt minds, incapable of accurately describing the faith, and rejected by those who genuinely understand the truth. Their impact will not be great (will not extend beyond the susceptible women) because the folly of the false teachers is apparent.

The text of 3:6-9 has been used in the development of some strange interpretations. The text is relatively clear in its teachings. Some people (in the text, some women) are especially susceptible to false teaching. False teachers usually work secretly, casting doubt and using mind-control methods. Those who oppose God's message and God's workers are not hard to identify. When they are identified and their teaching is refuted, their influence will be limited.

**3:10-17.** Paul's life presented a clear contrast to what had just been described. Timothy had followed (*parakoloutheo*, to follow closely, thus to know or to understand) Paul's teaching and life experiences. The aorist verbs show that Paul had already experienced these things—things Timothy was well aware of since he had often been Paul's traveling companion. The places mentioned in v. 11 were near Timothy's home town (see Acts 13, 14, 16). Paul was nearing the end of his life and was suffering hardship. He had endured persecutions and was able to write that God had delivered him. He did not expect that disciples would be exempt from suffering as they faithfully followed Christ. Through the centuries, persecution has come to Christians in many forms—not all physical. In Paul's view, the world is getting worse.

Verse 12 is for many a troublesome verse in our contemporary world where we experience few challenges in our Christian lives. "Everyone who wants to live for Jesus will be persecuted." Since we are reading occasional literature, this principle should first be applied to the specific first century context. In the context (3:1ff), this teaching may be Paul's analysis of what lies ahead for Christians in his day. That the text should be read as a general principle that applies in every situation is less probable. While it is true that the world and the Christian will always be in conflict, that conflict may not always rise to the level of physical persecution for all Christians today. Perhaps an application to the possibility of emotional, social, or economic persecution today is not beyond the scope of the text.

**3:14-17.** Because of the situation described in vv. 10-17, it was important that Timothy follow the teachings he had received (1:13, 2:1-2). The reference to the Holy Scriptures is to the Old Testament; the New Testament as a book did not yet exist at the time of Paul's writing. The reference to Timothy's childhood connects to 1:3-6. Paul affirms the inspiration of the Scriptures by God and their usefulness in four areas, resulting in the complete equipping of God's servants. The inspiration of Scripture affirms that the words of the Bible originated with God and not with human beings. The four verbs of v. 16 provide a progression: walking in the teaching (*didaskalia*), departing from the path and thus in need of rebuke (*elegchos*), correction (*epanorthosis*) that helps one return to the path, and instruction or training (*paideia*) for faithful living. The result is a Christian ready or complete (*artios,* perfect, ready) for service in every good work. The word *artios* is related to a word that means now or at this moment. The idea of "being ready" for every good work reflects the root idea. In this verse is the only occurrence of this word in the New Testament.

Paul has previously described the false teachers as unlikely to return to the faith, but he is concerned and hopeful that those who have been influenced by the false teachers will be restored. They need good teaching, rebuke when they err, correction that helps them return, and continual instruction.

## The Message of the Chapter Summarized

"With regard to false teaching and ungodly living, difficult days are coming. People will turn completely away from God, even though they will keep up enough appearance of religion to look respectable. In reality, their version of religion is powerless and you need to stay away from them!

"Some from this group are subtly influencing some of the women, especially those are always trying to understand how to live but are never able to understand enough to apply the word of truth. These 9i]'/modern-day false teachers are like the magicians who opposed Moses, but they will not succeed because their foolishness is obvious to all.

"You know all about my suffering for the gospel—my teachings, my life, my heart; you remember the sufferings that I endured in the cities near your home town, but God delivered me. People who want to live godly lives will suffer persecution, and evil people will get even worse, with more false teachers and more gullible people who will listen to anything. You must continue in what you have learned, the Scriptures that can give wisdom for salvation. The Scripture are inspired by God and useful for teaching, correcting, and maturing Christians so they are ready to do good works."

# 2 Timothy 4

*[Note: it is suggested that the student reread the introductory materials in this guide before beginning an individual preparatory reading and analysis. The process of general introductory reading, reading the context, reading the passage or text, outlining and paragraphing, and specific study should be used until it is a natural and normal part of Bible study. The goal is to make Bible study personal and to help the student develop her or his own skills in reading and understanding the Bible.]*

## CONTENT

The paragraphing included in the Content section of each chapter provides suggestions or guidance. The paragraphing and the descriptions of the contents will be helpful, but they are not the final word. The student is encouraged to identify the paragraphs and subsections within each paragraph to assist in his or her own study. After identifying the natural divisions in the text, the next step is to try to summarize the contents or message of each section.

The division of the biblical text into paragraphs is usually fairly standard in modern translations, but the descriptions of the contents often vary.

## Outline of the Chapter

| | |
|---|---|
| **4:1-5** | Paul's concluding instruction to Timothy about preaching and endurance |
| | *Note: these verses are a continuation of 3:10-17.* |
| **4:6-8** | Paul's awareness of and confidence in his situation |
| **4:11-16** | Conclusion and personal details |

## Observations about the Chapter

The paragraphs in this chapter are relatively easy to identify. Some versions make 3:10-4:5 a single paragraph that describes Paul's final charge to Timothy. I have divided that passage, maintaining the chapter division (3:10-17, 4:1-5) so that the study helps appear in the respective chapters.

## STUDY HELPS

**4:1-5.** Although this section is usually understood as a continuation of Paul's final instruction to Timothy, the command (*diamartureo*) is restated in 4:1. In 4:1-5, Paul includes nine imperatives in his instructions to Timothy. In 4:2 are five imperatives: Timothy is to preach (*kerusso*), to be prepared always (*ephistemi*), to correct (*elegcho*), to reprove (*epitimao*), and to encourage (*parakaleo*). (In some translations, the words used here parallel the list in 3:16, but in the original language only one of the four actions in 3:16 is repeated in this list.) Timothy is to do these things with a correct attitude, keeping in mind the challenges that will come. The rejection of healthy teaching will increase and become worse. Paul is describing the result of the false teachers and those who follow them. People will seek teachers who will say what they want to hear—an apt picture of the situation in many places and churches today. Continuing with four more imperatives (v. 5), Paul urges Timothy to respond to the threat of false teaching by distinguishing himself through his way of life. Be watchful (*nepho*), suffer hardship (*kakopatheo*, cf. 1:8), do (*poieo*) the work of an evangelist, and complete (*plerophoreo*) your ministry.

In 4:3 is the second use of the phrase "sound doctrine" in the Pastoral Letters (cf. 1 Tim. 1:10). The other two occurrences are in the book of Titus (1:9; 2:1).

**4:6-8.** Some have described these verses as Paul's final testament. The present tense verbs indicate that Paul could see that the things he describes were already occurring. Paul knew that his sacrifice was nearing completion; the time of his death was near. He confidently affirms that he has done three things: fought (*agonizomai*) the fight, finished (*teleo*) the race, and kept (*tereo*) the faith. He anticipates the crown (*stephanos*), the winner's wreath, that God will give him.

**4:9-22.** Only a few comments are necessary in these verses because they are easily understood. Few differences of opinion exist regarding these verses and the differing opinions are not of great importance for understanding the message of the paragraph.

**4:9-15**. Paul was in prison, desiring warmth and study materials, but the most pressing need for Paul was his desire to have his parchments (*membrana*, skins used for writing). These may have been materials Paul wanted to read or copies of things he had written.

**4:16-18.** Defense (*apologia*) is a technical word for a legal defense in the book of Acts. Paul frequently had to defend his actions. Paul writes that he stands alone with reference to men since many had deserted him, but that because God is always at his side he continues his work of declaring the gospel to the Gentiles, something he was able to do especially well in prison. The reference to being delivered to the lions is figurative, perhaps a way of saying that he has not yet been found guilty. Paul is confident God will continue to be with him and rescue him, even as he previously declared in 4:6-8. Throughout his life, this faith in God has been Paul's antidote to persecution and hardships. He is teaching Timothy about the faithfulness of God in order to prepare Timothy for difficulties and hardships.

**4:19-22.** As was often his custom, Paul concludes with personal greetings to several of those whom he knew. Paul often wrote the concluding part of a letter with his own hand (it was common to use a secretary or amanuensis to write the letter). In the concluding verse, the first you (your) is singular as is the word spirit. The second you is plural, again indicating that the letter was likely intended to be read to the church, even though the letter has numerous personal references and instructions. A public reading would serve to validate Timothy's actions in opposing the false teachers and would give him authority as Paul's representative and coworker. Understanding this purpose of the letter may also explain Paul's references to himself as an apostle (1:1, 11). One can identify throughout the letter various places where Paul's desire to give Timothy authority is in view (1:3-7; 1:8, 13-14; 2:1-2; 2:14; 3:14; 4:1-5).

## The Message of the Chapter Summarized

"Here is my solemn charge to you: preach, be persistent, correct, rebuke, and exhort; because the time is coming when people will not tolerate healthy teaching. They will seek what they desire, they will find teachers who will say what they want to hear, and they will constantly seek after new ideas. They will turn away from truth. You keep on doing your work: be moderate, suffer hardship, share the gospel, and complete your service.

"I have already completed my service and my departure is near. I have fought well, finished the race, and kept the faith, so I am confident of receiving God's crown.

"Please come as soon as you can. Many others have left me; only Luke is here. Bring Mark; bring my cloak and the scrolls. Alexander the coppersmith has been especially troubling in his vehement opposition to the message. No one stood by me in my defense, but God has continually been with me as I proclaim the gospel to the Gentiles. He delivered me, delivers me, and will deliver me. Many send greetings.

"The Lord be with your spirit. Grace to you."

# Titus 1

*[Note: it is suggested that the student read again the introductory materials in this guide before beginning any individual preparatory reading and analysis.]*

## CONTENT

The outlines and paragraphing in the Content section of each chapter only give suggestions and guidance. The student is encouraged to identify the paragraphs and subsections within each paragraph in his or her own study. The paragraphing in this chapter is fairly consistent in modern translations.

Outline of the Chapter
**1:1-4**     Greeting or salutation
**1:5-9**     The work of Titus on Crete
**1:10-16**   The work of elders, the importance of opposing
          false teachers

## STUDY HELPS

**1:1-4.** As is customary in the Greek letter form, the writer (Paul, bond-servant, apostle) and recipient (Titus, child in the faith) are mentioned in the greeting. Notice the focus on God in this paragraph—the word "God" appears five times in four verses. Paul's descriptions of himself as bond-servant (*doulos*) and apostle balance one another; one is a menial servant, the other is a person sent with authority. In the face of problems with false teachers, Paul desires to establish his credentials and authority. The letter is addressed to Titus but was intended also to be read to the church (the closing of the letter uses the plural form of "you" in 3:15).

Paul has been called to be an apostle and writes to strengthen the faith, knowledge, and hope of God's elect. The faith, knowledge and hope of the Christians on Crete are being endangered by false teachers who deny faith, distort knowledge, and eliminate hope. The knowledge of truth (see the same phrase in 2 Tim. 3:7) is according to or consistent with godliness. The modern tendency would be to reverse the order, godliness according to truth. Knowledge and truth are meaningless unless they result in godly living; godly living demonstrates the nature and power of the truth. Godliness depends on Jesus' identity (1 Tim. 3:16). Godliness is a common theme in the Pastoral Letters.

**1:2-3.** Faith depends on God's promises. God is faithful because of his unchanging nature. He cannot lie, so the promise he made long ago (before times eternal) remains in effect. The verb "promised" (*epaggello*) is aorist middle indicative, emphasizing the subject, God himself, and adding to the certainty of the promise. God's promises predate creation, but are now made known in God's own time (at the proper time) through the proclamation (*kerygma*) entrusted to Paul.

**1:4.** Titus was a companion of Paul; as a helper in Paul's ministry he had been entrusted with several difficult tasks. The lack of any reference to Titus in Acts is striking (see the Introduction). For parallels to the descriptive phrase in 1:4, see 1 Tim. 1:2; 2 Tim. 1:2, and Philemon 10. Paul and Titus shared a common faith.

The inclusion of "grace" and "peace" in the salutation reflects Paul's customary usage.

**1:5-9.** Paul names two tasks that had been entrusted to Titus on Crete: to set in order (*epidiorthoo*, to correct) the things lacking (*leipo*, to fail, to be absent, to lack, thus things left undone, deficient), and to set in place (*kathistemi*, to constitute, appoint, name) elders (*presbuteros*) in every city. "In every town" suggests the possibility that there was only one elder group in each city. Does this phrase mean that multiple house churches shared an eldership, or is it an indication that the church was not strong and that there was only one church or congregation in each city? The text does not answer the question.

We do not have details concerning the church on Crete before the time of this letter. Cretans were present in Jerusalem on Pentecost in Acts 2. The establishment of the church on Crete could have occurred as early as AD 30, shortly after the Day of Pentecost. We do not have any record of a visit by Paul to Crete

in the book of Acts, but Acts certainly has space for an unre-
corded visit by Paul, and it is also possible that other workers
were instrumental in beginning the church on Crete. No internal
evidence in the book of Titus helps us date the letter. (See the
Introduction for more on the historical background and the date
of the letter.)

Based on the contents of the letter, we know that there
was a deficiency in some aspects of the church, that there was a
Jewish element in the church, that problems had arisen with false
teaching, that some false teachers were seeking monetary gain
and were leading Christians away from the truth, and that there
were no elders. The lack of elders perhaps indicates a lack of
spiritual maturity.

**1:5-7.** The things deficient or lacking are not described
unless they are the problems that Paul mentions in the letter. The
leaders Titus was to appoint are described both as elders (1:5)
and overseers (1:7), almost certainly referring to one group. Acts
20 and 1 Peter 5 show that all three terms—overseer, elder, and
pastor—referred to one leadership group in the first-century
churches of the New Testament. Therefore, these verses give no
reason to suggest that Titus was to appoint two different groups
of leaders with two different functions, some as elders and others
as overseers. To appoint (*kathistemi*, to set in place) includes
delegating authority. The translation of v. 6 does not flow
smoothly in many translations. The first class condition can be
translated as "when." The result is: "I directed you to appoint
elders in every town when someone is above reproach, the husband of one wife...." This translation gives the sense of the
passage, especially in view of the repetition of "above reproach"
in v. 7.

The overseers are also described as stewards (*oikonomos*,
servants, sometimes translated as administrators). While it is
true that servants were sometimes given administrative respon-
sibilities, the concept of servant is too often lost in modern
understandings of this word. In the contemporary church where
leaders often tend to assume independent authority, two principles should be noted. First, overseers are responsible to another.
Second, overseers are not the owners of the house, they are

stewards responsible for the effective function of everything in the house.

The qualifications or characteristics of the leaders on Crete are somewhat different than those mentioned in Ephesus (see 1 Timothy 3). In a comparison of the two passages, one should keep in mind that the Pastoral Letters are occasional literature. The two lists served two different purposes. In Ephesus, elders were a part of the church organization as early as Acts 20 (c. AD 57), and in Paul's meeting with the elders as described in Acts 20, he predicted that problems would arise from among the elders in Ephesus. In view of the prediction Paul made in Acts 20, when Paul wrote to Timothy in Ephesus about five years later we can understand that the instructions about naming overseers were probably corrective. In the case of Titus on Crete, the text contains no indication that the church previously had elders, and it is more likely that we should see the list of characteristics as instructive. Good studies of the characteristics mentioned in these lists are available in other Bible study tools.

In light of the observations just made, several cautions are valid. The modern church must avoid using the lists in 1 Timothy 3 and Titus 1 as proof texts. The modern church must avoid the tendency to merge the two lists into one super list, thus obscuring the original context and purpose of the author and failing to understand the message of the books in the original context. The modern church must recognize the ambiguity, flexibility, and lack of absoluteness in the lists. Some of the descriptors are not measurable. For example, how hospitable must a church leader be? How does one measure hospitality?

**1:9.** Leaders are defined by what they do and how they act. Leaders hold fast (*antechomai*) the word of God. The word suggests the idea of holding something directly in front of oneself, of being "face to face" with the word of God. In modern terminology, the meaning is that God's leaders are constantly in touch with and are well versed in the word of God. They are focused on and continually confronted by the faithful word that is in accordance with the teaching. In this way, they will be able to teach what is consistent with God's word. Leaders are able to exhort and refute opponents. The opponents that were present on Crete are described in vv. 10-16. The work of opposing false teaching is not solely the responsibility of the preacher or evangelist. Spiritual leaders must be capable of teaching or explaining what the word says, exhorting (*parakaleo*) with sound (healthy) teaching, and refuting (*elegcho*, admonish, convict, convince, rebuke) false teachings.

**1:10-16.** The opponents are described as rebellious (*anupotaktos*, not willing to be in subjection), deceptive, and given to empty words and empty talk. They are empty talkers and mind misleaders. The group of false teachers may have been composed of both Gentiles and Jews, but Paul was especially concerned with the Jewish element, "especially those of the circumcision." These false teachers were influencing and misleading (*anatrepo*, literally, to overturn) entire families, seeking financial gain through their teachings, and disrupting the church. They were to be silenced by the work of the elders.

**1:12-14.** Paul cites a sixth-century BC Cretan named Epimenides to show how widespread certain problems were on Crete. The accusation has special force with reference to the false teachers. The false teaching was focused in Jewish myths and human commandments. The false teachers were to be reproved severely with the goal of returning them to sound teaching and truth. In v. 13, the goal is described as healthy (sound) faith. This passage could refer to the false teachers and the hope of restoring them, or to those who were being influenced by the false teachers. The main verb in v. 13 (*elegcho*, reprove or rebuke) is repeated in 2:15. Ideally, the translation of these two verses will note the repetition and will use the same word in the receptor language in both texts.

**1:15-16.** Verse 15 is likely a reference to asceticism, a belief system not specifically mentioned in Titus but clearly a factor in 1 Timothy and 2 Timothy—and also in Colossians, a book that belongs to the same general time period. Some, described here as defiled (*miaino*, contaminated, corrupted) and unbelievers, think that the way to follow God is to reject everything. "Nothing is pure; nothing is acceptable." They have both minds and consciences corrupted (*miaino*). With such false teachings, they profess to know God. They teach that self-denial is how one is brought closer to God. The result is most often the opposite. Paul says they deny God, being disobedient, detestable (*bdeluktos*, abominable, often used with regard to idolatry), and unfit for doing good (see also 2:14; 3:1, 8).

## The Message of the Chapter Summarized

"Paul a slave and apostle, to Titus my child in the common faith: grace and peace. I write to build up the faith, knowledge, godliness, and hope of God's chosen ones, since the promise of God that was made long ago has now been fulfilled and made a reality in this time. That is the message I am preaching.

"I left you in Crete to correct the things that were lacking and to name elders in every town—when anyone is above reproach and has a supportive family, because an overseer must be above reproach and be a good example of the Christian life. Above all, he must have the word of God always before him so he will be able to instruct others with healthy teaching and to rebuke those who teach against God's word.

"Many are not submissive; they are empty talkers and lead others away from the truth. These problems are especially prevalent among some of the Jewish believers. Such persons must be silenced because they are misleading entire families for financial gain. Even a Cretan philosopher has admitted that the Cretans struggle with telling the truth. This statement is true, and is obvious in the case of these opponents. Rebuke them sharply to bring them back to the faith, so that they will quit thinking about myths and fables and human commandments. Once people develop defiled thinking, they see everything as defiled. When people think pure thoughts, everything is pure. Although these false teachers claim to know God, because of their defiled thinking they are really denying God. They are detestable, disobedient, and unapproved with regard to any good work."

# *Titus 2*

*[Note: it is suggested that the student read the introductory materials in this guide before beginning an individual preparatory reading and analysis.]*

## CONTENT
The paragraphing included in the Content section of each chapter is provided only as a suggestion or model. The student is encouraged to identify the paragraphs and subsections within each paragraph as part of his or her own reading and study. In this chapter, the division of the biblical text into paragraphs is fairly consistent in modern translations.

Outline of the Chapter

| | |
|---|---|
| **2:1-10** | The responsibility of Titus to teach and model sound doctrine for various groups in the church |
| **2:11-14** | The gospel message summarized as motivation for Christian living |
| **2:15** | A summary of what Titus must do: reprove, speak, and exhort with authority |

*Note: the chapter naturally divides itself into two major paragraphs. It is easy in this chapter to identify smaller units of the text based on the various groups that are mentioned.*

## STUDY HELPS
**2:1-10**. This section contains references to different groups of people in the church: older men, older women, younger women, younger men (including Titus himself), and slaves. Based on the admonition in 2:1, the focus is on sound doctrine (healthy teaching). The use of this phrase in 2:1 is the last of only four occurrences of the phrase in the New Testament, all in the Pastoral Letters (1 Tim. 1:10; 2 Tim. 4:3; Tit. 1:9; 2:1).

      **2:1-2.** Paul tells Titus to speak (*laleo*) what is fitting for (consistent with) sound doctrine. This imperative controls vv. 2-5. The same verb is repeated in 2:15 (see comment at 1:13). The phrase, older men, does not refer to church leaders; the usage in this verse is parallel to 1 Timothy 5:1-2 and refers to the older men in the church. The things included in the list of instructions for the men are familiar in the study of the Pastoral Letters. The concluding admonition for the older men is that they are to be healthy in faith, love, and endurance (*hupomone*). The mention of "healthy faith" is repeated from 1:13. "Faith, love, and endurance" is unique; the usually expectation would be "faith, love, and hope."

**2:3-5.** The word "likewise" introduces the instructions that pertain to the older women. Paul gives instructions about what Titus should share with the older women, again speaking that which is consistent with sound doctrine. The concluding admonition for the older women is that they should be "teachers of good things."

The reason for the admonition is given in the first phrase of v. 4, "in order that...." The younger women are to be trained (*sophronizo*) by the older women. The younger women need to learn how to love their husbands and to love their children. These two things are often considered automatic in today's world, so the need to receive such instruction should catch our attention. The need for such teaching may reflect the negative impact of the false teachers in the homes (see 1:11, 2 Tim. 3:6-9). The younger women are to seek certain characteristics or qualities (v. 5), many of which parallel the instructions to the young widows in 1 Timothy 5. The phrase "subject to their own husbands" reflects Eph. 5:22-23 where the same teaching is given. The conclusion of v. 5 is the first of three parallel constructions: "so that...." Failure to live godly lives consistent with the word of God dishonors God's word.

---

"so that the message of God will not be blasphemed." 2:5
"so that the opponents will be confounded when they have nothing evil to say about us." 2:8
"so that the teaching about God our Savior will be adorned in every way." 2:10

---

**2:6-8.** "Likewise," introduces a new group. Titus is to exhort (*parakaleo*, encourage, urge) the young men. This verb controls vv. 6-10, and is repeated in 2:15. Some personal instructions for Titus are included in this section, perhaps suggesting that Titus was also a young man. Titus is to be an example of good works (cf. 1 Tim. 4:11). He is to preach a healthy message with honesty and sincerity. Godly living reinforces sound doctrine and combats false teaching since no accusations can be leveled against the Christians by those who oppose them.

**2:9-10.** The exhortation to slaves (*doulos*, bondservants) does not repeat the imperative. They are to be subject to their masters (parallel passages are in Eph. 6:5-9 and Col. 3:22-24). The instructions include submission, not arguing, not stealing, pleasing the masters, and acting always in good faith. For a parallel text in the Pastoral Letters, see 1 Tim. 6:1-2. By godly living, Christians adorn (*cosmeo*, to make attractive, the root of our word cosmetics) the doctrine (teaching) of God (teaching that is from God or is about God).

**2:11-14.** These verses are one sentence in Greek. Paul's purpose is to explain the reason and motivation for godly living. The passage may be an early creedal statement or faith formula. "For" connects these verses to the preceding commands. Godly living is always consistent with sound doctrine. The passage is built around a past-present-future progression.

Jesus came to bring salvation to all men (*anthropos*, all human beings, note the mention that God's plan for salvation includes everyone). "Grace of God" is a reference to the Incarnation. The grace of God appeared (*epiphaino,* past tense, compare our word epiphany). The present tense section of the sequence begins with the phrase "training us" (*paideuo*, to instruct, to train a child). The meaning of the word includes changes in knowledge and changes in action. Jesus' life, death, and resurrection change our way of living away from ungodliness toward sensible, righteous, and godly living. The instruction to deny ungodliness includes denying worldly desires, "in this present world."

"Looking for" (*prosdechomai*) is a present tense verb form but anticipates the future, looking forward to receiving.

"Appearing" is the noun form of the verb *epiphaino*. The reference is to the return of Jesus. The Greek construction means either "glorious appearing" or "appearing of glory," possibly referring to Jesus as the glory. Jesus is identified with God in this text, not meaning that Jesus is God the Father but that he is divine, having all of the characteristics of and nature of God.

**2:14.** He gave himself to redeem us and to cleanse or purify us. The phrase, "people for his own possession," reflects Exodus 19:5-7 where Israel is identified with the same wording in the Septuagint (LXX), translated as "God's treasure" in Exodus 19. The use of this word in this context reminds us of the Old Testament covenant relationship between God and his people. Israel belonged to God and to no other gods. God's people are zealous of good works (cf. 1:16; 2:3, 7, 14; 3:1, 8, 14).

**2:15.** The three verbs in this verse are repeated from earlier parts of the book: reprove from 1:13, speak from 2:1, exhort from 2:6. These are three active imperatives—keep on doing these things. This verse serves as a summary.

One of Paul's purposes in writing was to give Titus authority in the church on Crete. The last phrase in v. 15 is similar to 1 Tim. 4:12. In the context it may apply to the false teachers, or to believers who question Titus's authority to do the things mentioned in 1:5.

---

| 1:13 | Therefore <u>rebuke</u> them so they will be healthy in the faith |
| 2:1 | <u>Speak</u> the things befitting sound doctrine |
| 2:6 | <u>Exhort</u> the young men |
| 2:15 | These things <u>speak and exhort and rebuke</u> with all authority |

---

## The Message of the Chapter Summarized

"Speak the things that are consistent with sound doctrine. The older men must live right, sound in faith, love and endurance.

"Likewise, the older women must show fitting behavior, being teachers of what is good.

"In this way, they will be able to train the younger women in Christian living, so that the message will not be spoken evil of.

"Likewise, exhort the young men to be sober-minded. You yourself must be an example of good works that are consistent with your message, so that no one will have anything bad to say.

"Slaves should be subject to their masters, exhibiting genuine faith, so that the teaching about God our Savior is attractive.

"God's grace has appeared to bring salvation to the whole world, teaching us how to live in this world as we await his glorious appearing again. He gave himself to redeem us and purify for his possession a treasured people who are zealous of doing good.

"These things speak and exhort and rebuke with all authority so no one can despise you."

# *Titus 3*

*[Note: it is suggested that the student who is not yet familiar with the five-step Bible study process read again the introductory materials in this guide before beginning an individual preparatory reading and analysis.]*

## CONTENT
The paragraphing and descriptions included in the Content section of each chapter are merely suggestions or guides. The student is encouraged to identify the paragraphs and subsections within each paragraph as part of his or her own study, and to think about how the contents of each paragraph can be summarized in a heading. The division of the biblical text into paragraphs is usually fairly standard in modern translations; the headings often vary.

Outline of the Chapter
| | |
|---|---|
| **3:1-8** | Instructions for Christian conduct, possibly an early faith formula |
| **3:9-11** | Personal instructions for Titus |
| **3:12-15** | Final instructions |

Observations about the Chapter
This relatively short chapter falls into three primary paragraphs. Alternative paragraphing options appear in some studies. The reasons for the division of the text that is used here are explained in the study helps below.

## STUDY HELPS
**3:1-8.** This chapter brings together various themes from the letter. "Remind" with the use of the present tense verb indicates continued action—keep on reminding them. Remind is a frequent theme in the Pastoral Letters. The text of 3:1 connects with and continues the thought from 2:15. (Remember that the original letter did not have chapter divisions.) Titus is to continue to remind them of what they already knew.

Why Paul inserted the references to rulers and authorities is not clear. Perhaps his reference to the authority of Titus in 2:15 brought to mind the general principle that Christians live in subjection to authority. The reference can apply to both civil and spiritual authorities. "To be ready for every good deed" reflects a common theme in Titus.

---

## "GOOD WORKS" IN THE BOOK OF TITUS

*They profess to know God, but they deny him by their works. They are detestable, disobedient, unfit for any good work.* Titus 1:16

*Show yourself in all respects to be a model of good works, and in your teaching show integrity, dignity....* Titus 2:7

*...who gave himself for us to redeem us from all lawlessness and to purify for himself a people for his own possession who are zealous for good works.* Titus 2:14

*Remind them to be submissive to rulers and authorities, to be obedient, to be ready for every good work....* Titus 3:1

*The saying is trustworthy, and I want you to insist on these things, so that those who have believed in God may be careful to devote themselves to good works. These things are excellent and profitable for people.* Titus 3:8

*And let our people learn to devote themselves to good works, so as to help cases of urgent need, and not be unfruitful.* Titus 3:14

---

God is concerned with "all people" (cf. 2:11, 3:2). The actions described in v. 2, especially toward outsiders, will be a positive influence for the gospel.

**3:3.** The actions listed are characteristic of unredeemed humanity, perhaps suggesting that the application of v. 2 primarily has to do with the way Christians treat unbelievers.

**3:4-7.** These verses are one long sentence in Greek, possibly another early creedal statement (cf. 2:11-14). These two sections in the book of Titus (2:11-14 and 3:4-7) provide interesting contrasting descriptions of the gospel. In 2:11 "grace" appeared, here "kindness" appears.

In this paragraph, the main verb of the extended sentence, "he saved" (*sozo*, aorist tense), says that salvation is completed, not on the basis of (*ek*, out of) human actions but according to God's mercy. Justification is not by human merit; justification is by his mercy. God's mercy was made ours through the washing of regeneration, a reference to baptism, and the renewal that comes through the Holy Spirit. Acts 2:38 speaks of "baptism for remission of sins so that one receives the gift of the Holy Spirit." The parallel is easily seen. Much has been written with the intent of denying the plain meaning of the words Paul uses here.

He saved us through (*dia*, indicating instrumentality) the washing (*loutron*) of rebirth (*paliggenesia*, regeneration) and the renewing (*anakainosis*) of the Holy Spirit whom he poured out on us richly through Jesus Christ our Savior with the result that we are justified by his grace. "Having been justified by grace" (perfect participle, perfected or completed action) indicates that justification by grace comes after and is completed when the washing and the renewal have occurred. The goal of God's merciful salvation—salvation that is ours through washing and renewal that brings justification by grace—is that we can be heirs of eternal life.

---

*Faithful is the word: concerning these things I want you to constantly affirm so that those who have placed their faith in God will be careful to do good works.* --Titus 3:8

---

**3:8.** The trustworthy statement seems to refer to vv. 4-7, connecting v. 8 with what has just been said, "these things." This verse summarizes 3:1-7 and therefore is included in the first paragraph of the chapter (rather than making the paragraph division between v. 7 and v. 8). Titus is to teach these things so that believers will see opportunities and do good works, which is good and profitable for all people (*anthropos*). The repeated reference to "all people" provides a connection to vv. 1-7 since the instructions that follow apply primarily to Titus and use singular verb forms.

**3:9-11.** Avoid (*periistemi*, shun, stand away from) foolish inquiries (controversies), genealogies, quarrels and fights about the law. The reference to disputes about the Law may reflect problems with Jewish opponents and false teachers (cf. 1 Tim. 1:7-9; Tit. 1:9-11). Some people are naturally factious or divisive (*eris*). Such people are to be warned and rejected if they do not return to the faith. Many factious people are turning away (*ekstrepho*) rather than turning to (*epistrepho*) Christ. A similar form appears in 1:14 where false teachers turn from (*apostrepho*) the truth. Such people are sinners and self-condemned.

**3:12-14.** Artemas is not mentioned elsewhere in the New Testament. Tychicus is mentioned frequently (Acts 20:4; Eph. 6:21-22, Col. 4:7-8, 2 Tim. 4:12). Tychicus was the carrier of the letters Paul wrote from prison. Paul wanted Titus to leave Crete for the winter and spend the time with him at Nicopolis. In light of Titus's pending departure from Crete, even more obvious is that the letter was intended not only as a personal letter to Titus but also to inform the church (see 3:15). The situation described in v. 13 is unknown in other New Testament books. One final reference to good works caps this concluding section.

**3:15.** Paul's custom of sending greetings, his own greetings and greetings from those who were with him, is well known. The "you" in the final phrase is plural, suggesting that the letter was to be read to the entire church (or to the various churches in every city). See 1 Tim. 6:21, 2 Tim. 4:22 for parallels.

**The Message of the Chapter Summarized**

[2:15. These things speak and exhort and rebuke with all authority, so no one will despise you.]

"Remind them to be subject to all authority and to be ready for every good work, treating everyone right. We also used to live in conflict and hatred.

"When God's kindness and love appeared, he saved us not on the basis of our righteous works but according to his mercy, through the washing of rebirth and the renewal of the Holy Spirit whom he poured out richly on us, in order that we, having been justified, might be heirs of eternal life. Here is a dependable saying: teach these things so those who have faith in God will do good works. That benefits everyone.

"You must separate yourself from foolish theories, genealogies, quarrels, and fights about the law, because these accomplish nothing. Reject a divisive person after one or two warnings, knowing that such a one is turned away by sin and self-condemned.

"Here are my plans and what I would like you to do. Help those who come to help the church. In this way Christians can learn to do good works, to help with pressing needs, and not to be unfruitful. Greetings—from me, and from those with me. Grace be with all of you."

www.ingramcontent.com/pod-product-compliance
Lightning Source LLC
Chambersburg PA
CBHW071620040426
42452CB00009B/1415